Modern Workplace Culture Made Easy

Step-by-Step Strategies To:

Enhance Leadership

Build Inclusive Teams

Engage Remote Workers

SAGE LIFESTYLE
— PRESS —

Credits:

Cover art: Shefa R. @srumby17 (Freelancer.com)

Book images: Vector Mine http://www.vectormine.com

Contents

Introduction   V

1. Modern Workplace Culture   1

2. Developing Workplace Communication   9

3. Developing Leadership Skills   19

4. Building Trust and Accountability   27

5. Enhancing Team Dynamics and Collaboration   35

6. Cultural Transformation and Change Management   45

Make a Difference with Your Review   57

7. Measuring and Sustaining Cultural Success   59

8. Navigating Hybrid and Remote Work   69

9. Diversity, Inclusion, and Belonging   77

10. Addressing Pain Points and Challenges   85

11. Real-world Applications and Case Studies   95

12. The Future of Workplace Culture   103

Keeping the Game Alive   111

Conclusion   113

References   115

Introduction

L et's start with a story about a tech company on the brink of collapse. Lack of engagement among employees, high turnover rates, and stalled innovation characterized the company. But instead of accepting defeat, the leaders decided to transform the culture. They listened to their people, encouraged open dialogue, and fostered a sense of belonging. Within a year, employee engagement skyrocketed, and the company emerged as a leader in its field. This is the power of workplace culture—a silent force that can either propel organizations to new heights or drag them down.

Understanding and improving workplace culture is more than beneficial; it's vital for modern organizations. Statistics show that companies with solid cultures see higher employee satisfaction and better performance. A healthy culture leads to engaged employees who drive success. Culture is a company's invisible architecture, shaping how people interact, make decisions, and innovate.

Key Insights:

Companies with strong, positive cultures, like Zappos, Google, and Salesforce, report much lower turnover rates (often as low as 13.9%) and higher employee engagement than companies with negative cultures, where turnover can reach as high as 48.4%.

Companies with a great culture closely tie employee satisfaction to recognition, professional development opportunities, work-life balance, and feeling valued.

Today, workplace culture means more than ping-pong tables and free snacks. It includes how a company adapts to remote work, embraces diversity, and nurtures innovation. This book will guide you through these elements with actionable strategies and insights on how to create a culture supporting business goals and personal values.

This book covers several key themes. You'll explore leadership improvement and organizational development. You'll dive into modern workplace trends, including hybrid work environments. Each chapter is built on evidence-based frameworks and real-world case studies. You'll see what works and what doesn't in different settings.

Who will benefit from this book? Leaders, managers, and professionals who are serious about innovation and transformation. This book is for you if you struggle to balance high expectations with empathy or want to overcome challenges like low employee engagement. It avoids outdated methods and focuses on sustainable, long-term change, giving you reassurance and confidence that your efforts will yield lasting results.

Many organizations face common frustrations. Employees often feel disconnected from the company's purpose, and high expectations can lead to burnout. This book addresses these issues head-on and offers solutions that align with today's dynamic workplace realities. It integrates modern leadership practices with a focus on empathy and respect. We will introduce new concepts to you, such as scalability and empathy mapping. You'll discover the roles of thought leaders and disruptors in shaping culture. You'll feel equipped and prepared to initiate change in your organization.

As you read, expect to gain practical tools and strategies for cultural transformation. You'll learn how to become a thought leader in your field. This book will help you foster a thriving workplace culture that aligns with personal and professional values.

Finally, I invite you to take action. Start your journey of cultural transformation today. By embracing the concepts in this book, you can create a positive and lasting impact on your organization. You have the power to change the way your workplace functions, making it a place where everyone can thrive. Let's begin this journey together.

Chapter One

Modern Workplace Culture

"No company, small or large, can win over the long run without energized employees who believe in the mission and understand how to achieve it."-Jack Welch

Let's examine a well-established financial firm that faced a significant challenge: it was losing talented employees to startups that offered flexible work environments and inclusive cultures. The firm, which had traditionally operated with strict hierarchies and fixed office hours, strategically decided to remain competitive. They embraced remote work, encouraged diversity, and invested in technology to streamline operations. Implementing these changes was challenging, but the results were remarkable. Employee satisfaction soared, innovation thrived, and the company regained its competitive edge. This success story underscores the transformative power of redefining workplace culture in today's dynamic world, leading to increased employee satisfaction, enhanced innovation, and a stronger strategic position.

1.1 Defining Workplace Culture in Contemporary Settings

In the past, culture was often synonymous with hierarchy and conformity. A few people at the top made decisions, and everyone else followed suit. The focus was on maintaining the status quo. However, globalization reshaped these long-held norms as the world became more interconnected. Companies acknowledged the importance of varied demographics, thoughts, and innovation. This shift was driven by the need to adapt to rapidly changing markets and consumer expectations. The old ways of operating couldn't keep pace with the new global landscape, and so began the evolution of workplace culture. This evolution brings many benefits, from increased employee satisfaction to a more innovative and competitive business model, offering a bright and promising outlook for your organization's future.

Modern trends have further propelled this evolution. Hybrid work models that combine remote and in-office work, allowing employees flexibility and promoting work-life balance, have changed how we think about work. As per the Bureau of Labor Statistics, by 2023, roughly 60% of U.S. employees holding a four-year college degree or higher can now work remotely, at least part-time, showcasing a notable change in workplace dynamics. This model reduces attrition rates and increases employee satisfaction by offering greater flexibility. Technology, a key driver of this evolution, has become a cornerstone of modern workplace culture, facilitating communication across geographies and enabling seamless collaboration. These advancements have created a more inclusive work environment where diverse voices are heard and valued. Inclusivity is no longer a buzzword but a central theme defining successful organizations.

At the heart of contemporary workplace culture are core principles that guide organizations toward success. Integrity and transparency are foundational, fostering trust and accountability among team members. Collaboration and a shared vision ensure that everyone is aligned toward common goals, breaking down silos and encouraging cross-functional teamwork. In this constantly changing landscape, we must adopt the mindset of continuous learning and adaptability. Organizations prioritizing these values are better equipped to handle the complexities of the modern business landscape. They create environments where employees are empowered to innovate and contribute, driving personal and organizational growth.

However, redefining workplace culture has its challenges. Managing cultural change may feel daunting, especially when entrenched behaviors resist transformation. Leaders must be prepared to address these challenges head-on, fostering open communication and encouraging buy-in from all levels of the organization.

Yet, these challenges also present opportunities. Organizations embracing cultural diversity can leverage it for innovation, tapping into a rich tapestry of ideas and perspectives. By doing so, they stay relevant and position themselves as leaders in their respective industries.

1.2 Psychological Safety as a Cultural Cornerstone

Psychological safety is a term gaining traction in many workplaces today, yet its essence still needs to be discovered by some. Individuals in a psychologically safe environment are secure when expressing their ideas, questions, concerns, or mistakes without fearing negative consequences. This concept is pivotal because it lays the foundation for open communication and innovation. When employees believe they can speak up without retribution, creativity flourishes. In such environments, team members are likelier to share out-of-the-box ideas, challenge the status quo, and drive forward-thinking solutions that propel a company ahead of its competitors. This environment does more than encourage innovation; it actively drives it by removing the barriers of fear and judgment.

The benefits of fostering psychological safety extend beyond innovation. They significantly boost employee engagement, a critical factor in reducing turnover rates. Employees with a sense of safety are more engaged, believing that their contributions are significant and appreciated. This sense of value and belonging results in enhanced morale and loyalty. When people aren't worried about repercussions for speaking their truth or making mistakes, they're more likely to take calculated risks and push beyond their comfort zones, leading to personal and professional growth. Furthermore, a safe environment reduces the fear of failure, allowing mistakes to become learning opportunities rather than sources of shame or punishment. This shift in perspective can transform a workplace's culture into nurturing ground for growth and development.

Creating and maintaining psychological safety requires deliberate effort and strategy from leadership. One effective approach is establishing open-door policies, ensuring that leaders are accessible and approachable. This policy invites employees to share their thoughts and concerns openly. Regular feedback sessions also play a vital role. They provide structured opportunities for employees to voice their opinions and receive constructive input. These sessions should be frequent and part of the organization's routine to foster ongoing dialogue. Trust-building exercises can further solidify this foundation, encouraging team members to rely

3

on one another and work collaboratively. Simple activities, like team-building workshops or collaborative problem-solving sessions, can strengthen bonds and build trust over time.

However, the path to psychological safety has obstacles. Hierarchical barriers often pose a significant challenge. In many organizations, strict hierarchies can lead to environments where employees are hesitant to speak up due to perceived power dynamics. To conquer these barriers, leaders must actively work to dismantle them by advocating for egalitarian interactions and welcoming contributions from all levels of the organization. Another common obstacle is the fear of judgment. Employees may worry that their ideas or concerns could be met with ridicule or disapproval. Leaders can address this by fostering a culture of respect and empathy where diverse perspectives are welcomed and valued. Promoting a culture of constructive feedback instead of criticism can help ease this fear, leading to a more inclusive and open workplace.

Strategies for Cultivating Psychological Safety:

- **Encourage Open Communication:** Leadership should encourage open dialogue, where employees can share ideas, concerns, or mistakes without fear of punishment or humiliation. This is often fostered through regular feedback sessions and an open-door policy.

- **Inclusive Leadership:** Managers should actively listen to all voices and value input from all employees, regardless of rank or background. This also involves ensuring that diverse perspectives are encouraged and respected.

- **Non-punitive Responses to Mistakes:** Employees in psychologically safe workplaces are not blamed or penalized for making mistakes. Instead, mistakes are seen as learning opportunities, creating a culture of experimentation and continuous improvement.

- **Empathy and Support:** Leaders should demonstrate empathy and recognize their employees' emotional and mental wellbeing. This may involve offering mental health resources, promoting work-life balance, and maintaining open support lines.

- **Clear Behavioral Expectations:** Establishing and communicating clear, respectful guidelines for behavior helps employees know what is expected of them and ensures that inappropriate behaviors (like bullying or discrimination) are swiftly addressed.

Employees are more inclined to take risks and be innovative in a supportive, non-judgmental workplace. Leaders should promote a culture where taking thoughtful risks is rewarded, even if the outcomes are uncertain.

Psychological safety is a critical component of modern workplace culture that can increase innovation, engagement, and employee satisfaction. By understanding its importance and implementing strategies, organizations can create an environment where every voice is heard and every idea is valued.

1.3 The Role of Empathy Mapping in Team Dynamics

Empathy mapping is a tool that offers a window into the thoughts and emotions of team members, helping to illuminate their unique perspectives and needs. Originally from the world of design thinking, this visual technique captures and understands human experiences. Its purpose is to foster a deeper understanding of each team member by visualizing what they say, think, and do, providing insights into their emotions. This approach allows teams to step into the shoes of their colleagues, creating a shared understanding that transcends superficial communication. It also enables teams to uncover hidden insights that might remain unspoken, leading to more effective collaboration and problem-solving.

The "world of design thinking" refers to a problem-solving approach that centers on human needs and creativity. It's widely used in innovation, business, and product development to address complex issues by prioritizing empathy, ideation, prototyping, and testing. Design thinking combines creativity with strategic thinking to deliver user-friendly and practical solutions. Its concepts also encourage a mindset of experimentation, collaboration, and user-centricity. It's widely used in industries like technology, healthcare, education, and business for product development, service design, and innovation strategies. At its core, design thinking is about solving problems with empathy for the end user and applying creativity and logic to find solutions that work in real-life scenarios.

Initiating an empathy map requires the identification of team member personas. This involves gathering data about team members' roles, responsibilities, and challenges. Once the personas are established, the mapping process can start by filling in the empathy map's four quadrants: what the team members say, think, and do. This stage involves capturing direct quotes and observations about their communication and behavior. Additionally, the map explores their thoughts and feelings by considering what motivates or concerns them. Challenges they face are also noted, providing a complete picture of their experiences. By engaging in this process, teams can pinpoint disconnects or alignments between members' perceptions and reality, paving the way for targeted interventions that support individual and collective growth.

The benefits of empathy mapping are far-reaching, enhancing team communication, collaboration, and conflict resolution. Promoting a deeper understanding of diverse perspectives enhances the effectiveness of team communication. When team members are acknowledged and listened to, they are more inclined to share their ideas and participate in meaningful conversations. This improved communication also paves the way for better collaboration, as team members can anticipate and respond to each other's needs more effectively. Moreover, it aids in conflict resolution by identifying the root causes of disagreements and providing a framework for addressing them constructively. With a greater understanding of each other's viewpoints, teams can manage conflicts with empathy and find solutions that satisfy all parties involved.

Real-world examples illustrate the transformative impact of empathy mapping on team dynamics. Consider a marketing team at a global firm that struggled to align its creative efforts with client expectations. By implementing this process, the team could better understand the diverse perspectives within their group and the clients they served. This strategic move improved communication and collaboration, resulting in more cohesive campaigns and satisfied clients. Similarly, it helped bridge gaps between engineers and designers in a cross-functional team collaboration at a tech company. By visualizing each other's challenges and motivations, the team developed a shared language that facilitated smoother collaboration and more innovative solutions.

Empathy mapping surpasses mere tool status. Empathy mapping enhances individual and team performance and creates a more inclusive and supportive work environment. As modern organizations continue to understand and address the complexities of work in the 21st century, this tool offers a valuable approach to building resilient and cohesive teams that thrive on collaboration and mutual respect.

1.4 Elements of Empathy Mapping

An empathy map typically focuses on four quadrants:

1. **What Employees Think:** What are their thoughts on their work environment, tasks, or the organization? This might include worries, motivations, or ideas about future projects.

2. **What Employees Experience:** How do employees perceive their roles, relationships with coworkers, and organizational culture? This could reflect their emotional responses to challenges, successes, or stressors.

3. **What Employees Say:** What do employees verbalize in meetings, casual conversations, or feedback sessions? Their words provide clues to their levels of engagement and satisfaction.

4. **What Employees Do:** How do employees behave in their roles? Are they proactive, responsive, or disengaged? This quadrant focuses on their observable actions in the workplace.

Best Practices for Using Empathy Mapping

Conduct Employee Interviews and Surveys: To create accurate empathy maps, collect qualitative data through one-on-one interviews, anonymous surveys, or focus groups. This ensures that the map reflects real experiences.

Collaborate Across Teams: Involving multiple departments or team leaders in creating empathy maps ensures that insights are well-rounded and account for different perspectives within the organization.

Use the Empathy Map to Improve Communication: After mapping out employee experiences, use the insights found to improve communication between leadership and staff. Adjust messaging to be more empathetic and reflective of employees' actual concerns and needs.

Align with HR and Leadership Strategies: Empathy maps should inform broader strategies for employee wellbeing, mental health, and career development. Leadership can use these insights to make data-driven decisions about workplace policies, professional growth opportunities, and employee support systems.

Iterate and Revisit Regularly: This is not a one-time process. As employee experiences and workplace dynamics evolve, companies should update empathy maps periodically to reflect current insights.

Encourage a Culture of Continuous Feedback: To maintain the relevance of the empathy map, foster continuous feedback loops where employees are comfortable sharing their thoughts and feelings. This ensures that the empathy map evolves with their needs and the company culture.

Chapter Two

Developing Workplace Communication

"Communication is the real work of leadership."– Nitin Nohria

E nvision a team where every member is genuinely connected to their leader—not just because of their title or authority but for their authenticity and openness. The significance of authentic leadership has never been more evident. It emerged prominently with Bill George's work, underscoring the importance of integrity and stewardship in leadership roles. Authentic leaders are keenly aware of their core values and moral compass, fully understanding the environment in which they operate. Rather than simply fulfilling a role, they live out their beliefs and consistently align their actions with those values. This alignment is what makes them genuine, and their authenticity is what inspires those around them.

2.1 Authenticity and Vulnerability

Authentic leaders possess specific defining characteristics. They have a clear sense of purpose and lead with their heart, showing compassion and empathy. They build strong relationships, demonstrating self-discipline and consistency in their actions. These leaders are self-aware, understand their strengths and weaknesses, and practice solid values, ensuring their actions align with their beliefs. Vulnerability is a critical component of authentic leadership. It's about being open, admitting mistakes, and showing genuine emotions. This doesn't weaken a leader's position but strengthens their connection with their team, fostering a culture of trust and mutual respect.

Leadership vulnerability transforms team dynamics. When leaders are transparent about their challenges and uncertainties, they build a bridge of trust with their team members, which is the foundation of effective leadership. It encourages team members to be open, share their thoughts, and collaborate without fear. Upon recognizing their leader as human, team members establish a stronger connection and commitment to the team's goals. This openness creates a safe space for innovation and creativity, as people are not afraid of making mistakes or facing criticism.

Leaders can take several practical steps to embrace vulnerability while maintaining authority. Participating in personal stories and sharing challenges is a potent way to create connections. Leaders can share their struggles and learning experiences openly with their teams. Talking about how they've conquered personal or professional obstacles demonstrates their humanity. This creates trust and encourages employees to be open about their difficulties and needs. Sharing personal anecdotes is more than just a tactic; it's a means to promote a stronger connection and understanding within the team. Another effective strategy involves fostering open discussions about failures. Leaders must create an environment where failures are seen as learning opportunities rather than setbacks. This approach builds trust and promotes a culture of continuous improvement.

Vulnerability Exercise

A workplace vulnerability activity promotes trust, openness, and connection within a team by encouraging employees and leaders to share personal insights in a safe and supportive environment. Here's an example activity.

- **Begin by Creating a Safe Space:** Establish ground rules for confidentiality and respect to ensure everyone is secure when sharing personal stories. Vulnerabilities shared in the session must stay confidential.

- **"Two Truths and a Challenge" Exercise:** In this activity, participants share two personal strengths or truths about themselves and one challenge they currently face, whether at work or in life. Participants can reflect on their capabilities and establish security in recognizing areas needing support. For example, a team member might share that they are a good problem solver and a supportive team player, but they currently need help with time management due to personal commitments.

- **Leader-led Exercise:** Leaders can model vulnerability by starting the session with personal stories about challenges, mistakes, or lessons learned in their careers. This sets a tone of openness, showing employees that sharing difficult experiences is okay. Leaders empower their team members to do the same by leading the exercise.

- **"Fail Forward" Storytelling:** Each participant shares a story about a failure or mistake they've made in their career and what they learned from it. The group creates an environment where risk-taking is encouraged by normalizing failure and turning it into a learning experience.

Create a platform where employees can give anonymous feedback about their vulnerabilities or what they think could make the workplace more supportive. Analyzing and discussing this feedback can result in taking actionable steps toward constructing a more empathetic culture.

Best Practices:

- Encourage leaders to participate actively in modeling the behavior they wish to see.

- Maintain psychological safety throughout the activity by ensuring nobody is pressured to overshare.

- Show appreciation and acknowledgment in the workplace to strengthen these lessons.

There are abundant real-world examples of leaders who successfully incorporate vulnerability into their leadership style. Consider the case of a CEO who, during a critical downturn, was completely transparent with her team about the company's challenges. She shared her fears and uncertainties, as well as her unwavering belief in the team's ability to overcome them. Her vulnerability inspired the team to rally together, leading to a remarkable turnaround. Participating in personal storytelling and engaging in trust-building activities helped break down barriers and foster stronger connections within the team.

By embracing these principles, leaders can foster environments where trust, loyalty, and open communication thrive, laying the groundwork for enduring success. These practices enhance team dynamics and improve performance and innovation, creating a more cohesive and productive work environment.

2.2 Mastering Transparent Communication with Teams

Transparent communication is the backbone of any successful organization. It's about clarity, openness, and trust. When communication is transparent, employees understand the business' current state, strategy, and their role within that framework. This understanding leads to more engagement, effectiveness, and a sense of purpose. Employees are, then, more likely to align their tasks with the company's goal of having a cohesive work environment. Transparency also enhances accountability, as everyone knows what's expected of them and how their contributions fit into the larger picture. This clarity of purpose drives motivation and performance, creating an environment where innovation thrives.

Effective, transparent communication is comprised of several key elements. First, clarity in messaging is vital; messages must be straightforward and free of jargon that could confuse or mislead others. Consistency in information sharing is equally important. Employees should receive regular updates about the company's objectives, progress, and any changes that might affect them. This regularity builds confidence and trust, as employees perceive themselves as informed and involved. Openness to feedback is another component of creating a culture where employees are open to sharing their input.

Open forums for questions and feedback are also beneficial. These forums provide a platform for employees to voice their opinions and ask questions in a safe space, encouraging dialogue and mutual understanding. Their active participation and response to feedback demonstrate their commitment to transparency and inclusivity, further strengthening trust within the team.

Transparent communication might create the unwanted result of communication silos. These silos occur when departments or teams operate in isolation, withholding information that could benefit others. To address these barriers, leadership must consciously foster collaboration between departments and share information. Another challenge is balancing transparency with confidentiality. Sometimes, sensitive information cannot be shared openly due to privacy or legal concerns. Leaders must overcome this delicate balance carefully, ensuring they are as transparent as possible while respecting necessary boundaries. This balance can be achieved by being clear on what can be communicated, which helps maintain trust even when full disclosure isn't possible.

2.3 Engaging Remote Teams through Effective Dialogue

Remote work has become a staple in modern workplaces, bringing unique challenges that can impact how teams communicate and stay engaged. Communication barriers often arise in virtual environments, primarily due to the lack of face-to-face interaction. These barriers can lead to misunderstandings, as non-verbal cues are more complicated to interpret through a screen. Additionally, maintaining engagement with remote team members can be challenging, as team members may experience isolation or disconnection from their colleagues. This sense of detachment can breed feelings of disconnection from the team's objectives, leading to decreased motivation and productivity. As a leader or team member, try to recognize these challenges and actively work to bridge the gap, ensuring the team's spirit and cohesion remain strong.

Several strategies can be implemented to facilitate meaningful and productive communication with remote teams. Scheduling regular video check-ins is a powerful way to keep everyone aligned and maintain a sense of camaraderie. These check-ins don't have to be long; even brief, focused meetings can help keep everyone on track and allow team members to voice concerns or share updates. Collaborative communication tools like Slack or Microsoft Teams can enhance dialogue, allowing real-time communication and project collaboration. These platforms enable teams to share ideas, provide feedback, and work together seamlessly, regardless of physical location.

By leveraging technology, remote teams can mimic some of the dynamics in traditional office settings, fostering more dynamic interactions.

Maintaining inclusivity in remote communication is essential, demanding thoughtful practices to ensure all team members are heard and valued. Encouraging participation from every team member, regardless of their role or time zone, is vital for fostering an inclusive environment. Leaders should consciously solicit input from quieter team members during meetings, ensuring diverse perspectives are considered. Additionally, addressing diverse communication styles is essential. Some team members may prefer written communication over verbal—or vice versa. Flexibility and accommodating different preferences help bridge communication gaps and foster a more inclusive atmosphere.

Real-world examples illustrate the success of these strategies. Consider a tech company that faced challenges in keeping its remote teams engaged. The company strengthened connections among team members by implementing regular virtual team-building activities. These activities, ranging from online trivia games to virtual coffee breaks, provided a casual space for employees to interact and bond. The result was a more cohesive and motivated team, with improved communication and collaboration. Another case study involves a company successfully using collaborative tools to maintain engagement. By incorporating project management software and video conferencing, the team could keep projects on track and maintain a high level of engagement, even when working miles apart. These examples demonstrate that, with the right strategies, remote teams can overcome communication challenges and achieve remarkable success.

2.4 Feedback Loops: Constructive Communication Techniques

In today's workplaces, feedback loops support continuous improvement. At their core, feedback loops are structured processes that allow for regular input and reflection within teams. They serve as channels for open communication, enabling employees to understand their performance and identify areas for development. The purpose is to critique and foster an environment where continuous learning and improvement are embraced. Effective feedback loops ensure that communication flows in both directions, allowing team members to provide and receive insights that drive personal and organizational growth. Constructive feedback can enhance team performance by pinpointing strengths and addressing weaknesses.

In employee engagement, a feedback loop refers to the continuous process of gathering input from employees, analyzing that feedback, and then taking action to improve the work environment, leadership practices, or organizational culture based on that input. It creates a cycle where employee opinions are heard and acted upon, promoting a culture of openness and responsiveness.

Here's how it works:

- **Collect Feedback:** Employees provide feedback through surveys, one-on-one meetings, or performance reviews. This feedback may relate to job satisfaction, management, work processes, or workplace culture.

- **Analyze Feedback:** Leaders or HR teams assess the input to identify trends, challenges, or areas of concern. For example: if employee's express frustration with unclear communication, this issue is recognized as a critical area to address.

- **Take Action:** Based on the feedback, the company implements changes, such as improving communication channels, providing more training, or introducing new employee recognition programs.

- **Follow-up and Feedback Again:** After changes are made, further feedback is gathered to see if the actions have positively impacted. This loop continues, allowing for constant improvement in employee engagement.

Effective feedback loops build trust between employees and management because they show that employee input leads to meaningful change, thus fostering higher engagement and satisfaction.

Employees receiving regular, actionable feedback can make informed decisions about their work, improving outcomes. Furthermore, feedback loops enhance team morale and motivation. When team members feel their contributions are recognized and valued, their engagement and satisfaction increase. This recognition facilitates a culture of trust and respect, where employees are more inclined to take initiative and innovate. When executed well, feedback loops create a positive cycle where performance and morale reinforce one another.

To deliver feedback effectively, leaders can employ several practical techniques. For example, the "sandwich" feedback technique involves constructive criticism sandwiched between positive affirmations. This method softens criticism's impact, leaving the recipient encouraged, not discouraged. Regular 360-degree feedback sessions are another valuable tool. These sessions provide a comprehensive view of an employee's performance by gathering input from peers, subordinates, and supervisors. This holistic approach ensures that feedback is well-rounded and balanced, offering diverse perspectives on strengths and areas for growth.

Creating a feedback-friendly environment is also important. Leaders should encourage open dialogue; members must feel legitimately safe expressing their ideas without fear of retribution. This openness advances a culture of continuous feedback where learning and development are prioritized.

Implementing feedback loops can come with challenges. Resistance to feedback is a common obstacle, often stemming from fear of criticism or defensiveness. To overcome this, leaders must emphasize the developmental nature of feedback, framing it as an opportunity for growth rather than judgment. Ensuring feedback is both actionable and specific is another challenge. General feedback that lacks specificity can result in employees being confused or undervalued. To address this, leaders should provide clear examples and tangible suggestions for improvement, ensuring that feedback is meaningful and practical. By focusing on specific behaviors and outcomes, feedback becomes a tool for empowerment rather than critique.

Best Practices for Implementing Feedback Loops

- **Create Multiple Channels for Feedback:** Provide various ways for employees to share feedback, such as one-on-one meetings, anonymous surveys, suggestion boxes, or digital platforms. This guarantees that all voices can be heard, regardless of personal communication styles or comfort levels.

- **Encourage Regular Feedback, Not Just Annual Reviews:** Replace or complement annual performance reviews with ongoing feedback cycles. Regular feedback sessions ensure timely insights and allow for quick course corrections.

- **Be Transparent About the Process:** After gathering feedback, share with employees what was heard and how the organization plans to act on it. Transparency builds trust and shows that the feedback loop is taken seriously.

- **Empower Leaders and Managers with Feedback Skills:** It's crucial to equip managers with the skills to give and receive feedback effectively. This includes the ability to seek constructive criticism, listen actively without defensiveness, and foster a psychologically-safe environment where feedback is valued.

- **Act on Feedback to Complete the Loop:** Acknowledge the feedback, make necessary changes, and communicate those actions to the team. Remember, as a leader, your role in the feedback loop is crucial. Failing to close the loop can result in disengagement or mistrust, so it's important to take feedback seriously and act on it.

- **Normalize Feedback in Daily Operations:** Develop a culture where feedback is part of daily interactions, not just a formality. Regular, informal check-ins can make the process more natural and less intimidating, fostering a culture of continuous improvement.

- **Monitor and Adjust the Process:** Continuously assess the feedback loop. Is it effective? Are employees engaged with it? Make adjustments as needed to ensure it continues to improve communication, performance, and workplace culture.

Create an environment where feedback drives continuous improvement, furthers collaboration, and enhances employee satisfaction.

Chapter Three

Developing Leadership Skills

'Leadership is the art of getting someone else to do something you want done because he wants to do it.' – Dwight D. Eisenhower

P icture a bustling open-plan office filled with the hum of keyboards and the murmur of conversations. At the center of this dynamic environment is a leader who manages the complexities of tasks and team dynamics effortlessly. This leader is not only relying on technical skills or authority. Instead, they wield a powerful tool: emotional intelligence (EI). The ability to understand and manage emotions—both their own and those of others—has set them apart. EI is increasingly recognized as essential for leadership success, often more significant than traditional measures of intelligence. It enables leaders to connect, inspire, and drive their teams toward shared goals.

3.1 Emotional Intelligence

Let's discuss the key components of EI needed for effective leadership.

- **Self-awareness:** Employees and leaders can assess their strengths and weaknesses, respond effectively to feedback, and understand how their emotions impact their performance and relationships.

- **Self-regulation:** In the workplace, individuals with solid self-regulation remain calm under pressure, avoid reactive behavior, and demonstrate adaptability to changes or stressors.

- **Motivation:** Emotionally intelligent individuals are motivated not just by external rewards like salary but by internal values such as personal growth, achievement, or the desire to contribute meaningfully to projects. Motivated employees are more productive, resilient, and committed to their goals, even when facing challenges.

- **Empathy:** Practicing empathy involves actively listening and recognizing colleagues' emotional cues. Empathetic employees and leaders are better at building relationships, managing team dynamics, and fostering an inclusive and supportive workplace environment.

- **Social Skills:** Employees with strong social skills are adept at networking, working in teams, and leading others positively. They are often seen as excellent team players or leaders who can inspire and engage their peers.

These components of EI impact individual and organizational success in the workplace by fostering a culture of trust, resilience, and collaboration. Leaders with high EI can build strong interpersonal relationships, become the cornerstone of effective teams, and create an environment where employees can be heard and appreciated. This openness advances collaboration and innovation, driving the team toward success. Moreover, leaders with high EI are adept at navigating complex social dynamics. They can manage conflicts with empathy, turning potential disruptions into opportunities for growth and unity. The transformative power of EI in leadership should inspire and motivate you to further develop your EI skills, as they can lead to a more engaging, productive, and harmonious work environment.

Self-assessment tools are an excellent starting point to identify strengths and areas for improvement. These tools provide valuable insights into one's emotional landscape, setting the stage for growth. Mindfulness and meditation practices are also effective in cultivating self-awareness and self-regulation. Leaders can manage their emotions and respond to challenges with clarity and calm by taking time to reflect and center themselves. Empathy exercises and role-playing are additional techniques to connect with others. Leaders can build empathy and improve social skills by stepping into different perspectives, ultimately strengthening their leadership capabilities.

Real-world examples highlight the transformative power of EI in leadership. Consider the case of a manager who successfully used EI to resolve a conflict between two team members. The manager facilitated a solution that satisfied everyone involved by listening empathetically to both sides and acknowledging their concerns. This approach, guided by emotional intelligence, not only resolved the immediate issue but also strengthened the team's cohesion and trust. It's a clear demonstration of how EI can be a powerful tool in maintaining a harmonious and productive team environment.

Emotional Intelligence Self-assessment

- **Reflect on Your Emotions:** Spend a few minutes each day reflecting on your emotions and how they influence your actions.

- **Mindfulness Practice:** Dedicate time to mindfulness exercises, such as deep breathing or meditation, to enhance self-awareness and regulate emotions effectively.

- **Empathy Exercise:** Participate in a role-playing activity where you assume a team member's perspective. Consider their challenges and motivations to build empathy and understanding.

3.2 Building Future Leaders

Envision a tree's roots buried deep and the supporting branches reaching the sky. This tree symbolizes a leadership pipeline within an organization, a structured path for developing future leaders who will eventually help and grow the company. This pipeline is a strategic approach to leadership development that identifies and nurtures potential organizational leaders. It ensures the continuity of leadership and prepares the organization for future challenges. By identifying potential leaders early and encouraging their growth, a leadership pipeline enables them to take on more significant roles when the time is right. This proactive approach avoids the scramble for leadership talent when vacancies arise, ensuring a seamless transition and maintaining organizational stability.

Mentoring goes beyond simply sharing knowledge and into cultivating future leaders with the confidence and decision-making skills necessary to succeed. Through mentoring, seasoned leaders pass on their expertise and insights to emerging leaders, accelerating their growth by providing wisdom and lessons that might, otherwise, take years to learn. This exchange boosts the mentees' development and ensures the continuity of strong leadership within the organization. The relationship also builds confidence, allowing mentees to take on challenges with the assurance that they have a mentor to guide and support them. Decision-making abilities are honed as mentees learn to analyze situations and consider various perspectives, often with the mentor providing valuable feedback and advice.

For a mentoring program to be effective, it must be thoughtfully designed and implemented. Start by matching mentors with mentees based on their goals and skills. This alignment ensures that the mentoring relationship is mutually beneficial, with both parties learning and growing. Outlining clear objectives and expectations at the beginning is also essential. This clarity helps both mentor and mentee stay focused and measure progress. Regular feedback and progress assessments are essential components of a successful program. These sessions provide opportunities to reflect on achievements and assist in making improvements and adjustments. Identify areas for improvement and adjust goals as needed. By maintaining open communication, the mentoring relationship remains dynamic and responsive to the evolving needs of the mentee.

Successful leadership pipelines are not theoretical; they exist in various organizations and have proven effective. For instance, a multinational corporation has embedded mentorship into its culture. This company pairs seasoned leaders with emerging talent, creating a structured program focusing on personal and professional development. Mentors meet regularly with their mentees, offering guidance and support. The impact is clear: the company benefits from a steady stream of capable leaders well-prepared to step into leadership roles.

Similarly, a non-profit organization has developed a unique approach to nurturing future leaders. Acknowledging the necessity of diverse viewpoints, the organization established cross-functional mentoring teams to encourage collaboration and innovation. The result is a leadership pipeline that prepares individuals for future roles and enriches the organization's culture with fresh ideas and perspectives.

Mentoring and leadership development are about building a resilient and adaptable organization. By investing in the growth of future leaders, organizations ensure their continued success and relevance in an ever-changing world.

3.3 Accountability in Leadership: A Framework

Accountability in leadership is like the backbone of a thriving organization. When leaders hold themselves and their teams accountable, it creates a foundation of trust and performance excellence. Accountability is about setting clear expectations and responsibilities which provide a roadmap for individuals to follow. When everyone knows their role and what is expected, ambiguity is eliminated and sense of ownership is strengthened. Leaders who prioritize accountability ensure that their teams understand the outcomes they are responsible for, which motivates them to strive for success. This clarity is important; it sets the stage for excellent performance and instills confidence in the team's abilities to meet and exceed goals.

The benefits of accountable leadership are manifold. Leaders who want an environment of trust consistently hold themselves and their teams accountable. Trust is the glue that binds a team together, enhancing cohesion and reliability. When team members trust each other and their leader, they are more engaged and committed to their work. This trust improves decision-making and problem-solving, as individuals are empowered to share ideas and take risks. In an accountable environment, teams are more agile, quickly deal with challenges, and produce results that align with the organization's objectives. The ripple effect of this trust extends beyond the team, positively impacting the entire organization.

Specific strategies and tools can be implemented to foster accountability within leadership practices. Accountability check-ins and progress reviews effectively maintain focus and ensure everyone is on track. These regular sessions provide opportunities to discuss achievements, address challenges, and realign objectives, if necessary.

Creating a culture of transparency and openness is also essential. Leaders should encourage open dialogue, allowing team members to share their thoughts and concerns comfortably. This openness builds mutual respect and understanding, reinforcing the commitment to accountability. Promoting peer accountability and support further bolsters this culture. When team members hold each other accountable, they strengthen the collective responsibility for success and create a supportive environment where everyone is invested in achieving common goals.

Examples of accountability in action demonstrate its powerful impact on leadership and team performance. Consider a software company that implemented an accountability-driven approach to project management. By clearly defining roles and responsibilities and conducting regular progress reviews, the company could deliver projects on time and within budget. This accountability framework improved project outcomes and enhanced team morale and collaboration. In another instance, a financial institution adopted accountability frameworks to strengthen its leadership practices. By embedding accountability into its culture, the institution saw significant improvements in decision-making and problem-solving, leading to increased profitability and customer satisfaction. These examples illustrate that when accountability is prioritized, it transforms leadership and drives organizational success.

Accountability Checklist

- **Set Clear Expectations:** Outline your team's roles, responsibilities, and desired outcomes.

- **Regular Check-ins:** Schedule consistent progress reviews to discuss achievements and challenges.

- **Encourage Openness:** Cultivate a culture where team members can easily share feedback and concerns.

- **Encourage Peer Support:** Promote an environment where team members hold each other accountable.

Accountability is a critical component of effective leadership. By implementing these strategies and fostering a culture of accountability, you can enhance your leadership practices and drive your team's performance to new heights.

3.4 Resilience as a Leadership Competency

Imagine standing in a whirlpool of chaos, but calm prevails at the center. This is the essence of resilience. It allows leaders to maintain a steady course despite unexpected disruptions. Resilient leaders are not immune to difficulties but possess the agility to handle them, emerging more focused. This capability is vital in today's fast-paced, ever-evolving business landscape, where constant change and uncertainty are the norm.

Resilient leadership offers numerous benefits that contribute to long-term success and stability. One of its primary advantages is sustaining motivation and focus during difficult times. Resilient leaders inspire their teams to persevere when challenges arise, keeping morale high and objectives clear. This unwavering dedication ensures teams remain productive and engaged, even when faced with setbacks. Furthermore, resilient leaders encourage a similar mindset within their teams. By modeling resilience, they instill a culture of tenacity and adaptability, empowering team members to confront challenges head-on. This collective resilience enhances individual performance and strengthens the team's cohesion and effectiveness.

Building resilience is an achievable goal for leaders, and several strategies can help develop it. Stress management and coping strategies are vital components of resilience. Further, exercise and deep breathing are ways to manage stress and maintain clarity under pressure. These practices enable leaders to approach challenges with calmness and poise, fostering a sense of stability within their teams. Building a support network and seeking mentorship is another effective strategy. By surrounding themselves with trusted advisors and mentors, leaders can gain valuable insights and perspectives, bolstering their resilience. These relationships provide a safety net of guidance and encouragement, helping leaders confidently work through complex situations. Embracing failure as a learning opportunity is essential. Resilient leaders view setbacks not as defeat but as chances for growth and improvement. By analyzing and learning from failures, they refine their strategies and emerge better equipped to face future challenges.

Real-world examples highlight the pivotal role of resilience in leadership. Consider the case of a CEO who led their company through an organizational crisis. Faced with financial difficulties and declining morale, the CEO demonstrated resilience by maintaining transparency and open communication with employees. By addressing concerns and outlining a clear recovery plan, the CEO inspired confidence and unity within the organization. This resilient leadership stabilized the company and positioned it for renewed growth and success. In another example, a business needed to pivot its strategies due to market shifts. Guided by resilience, the leadership team embraced the change, adapted their approach, and achieved new levels of success and relevance in their industry.

Resilience is a vital leadership competency that empowers leaders to tackle challenges with strength and determination. Leaders can foster a supportive and adaptable work environment by cultivating resilience within themselves and their teams. This foundation drives individual and organizational growth and prepares leaders for the complexities of an ever-changing world. In the next chapter, we will explore how these leadership competencies integrate with modern workplace trends, shaping the future of work and organizational success.

Chapter Four

Building Trust and Accountability

"Accountability is the glue that ties commitment to the result." – Bob Proctor

W orkplace accountability requires taking responsibility for one's role and understanding how individual actions contribute to the organization's success. Ownership—a potent concept—denotes individuals' commitment to their work. It's about seeing a project through from start to finish, taking pride in its outcome, and understanding its impact on the team's broader goals. This ownership goes beyond mere responsibility. It's an empowerment. It gives individuals control over their work and instills confidence in their abilities. While accountability ensures that tasks are completed, ownership inspires individuals to go above and beyond, fostering a culture of excellence and dedication.

4.1 Accountability and Ownership

The interplay between ownership and accountability is essential for enhancing team performance. Accountability establishes a system where individuals answer for their actions, creating a framework of reliability and predictability. At the same time, ownership fuels passion and drives innovation. These concepts establish a dynamic in which team members are accountable for their contributions and driven to surpass expectations. This synergy leads to improved performance, as employees are more engaged and invested in their work, resulting in higher productivity and efficiency.

A culture of accountability brings numerous benefits that extend beyond individual performance. When accountability is embedded in the organizational ethos, it leads to increased employee engagement. Employees with a sense of accountability are more inclined to take proactive and participative actions, which adds to the liveliness and dynamism of the work environment. This engagement translates into enhanced productivity, as team members are more focused and efficient in their tasks. Additionally, a culture of accountability creates trust among team members. All adhere to the same standards in this culture. Setting clear expectations for all ensures a fair playing field where merit and effort are acknowledged and compensated. This recognition reinforces a positive feedback loop, further boosting morale and motivation.

Cultivating ownership among team members requires deliberate strategies and actions. One practical approach is establishing clear goal-setting and personal accountability frameworks. By setting specific, measurable, achievable, relevant, and time-bound (SMART) goals, team members can track their progress and hold themselves accountable for meeting objectives. This clarity provides a roadmap for success, guiding individuals toward their desired outcomes. Recognition and reward systems are also powerful tools for encouraging ownership. Acknowledging and celebrating achievements through verbal praise, bonuses, or other incentives reinforces the value of taking ownership and enhances employees' sense of appreciation and worth, motivating individuals to continue striving for excellence.

Fostering accountability has its challenges, especially when one fears failure or embarrassment. These feelings can hinder individuals from stepping up and taking responsibility. To overcome this fear, it is essential to create a supportive environment where mistakes are viewed as learning opportunities rather than setbacks.

As a leader, you can help individuals embrace accountability without fear of repercussions by encouraging open communication and providing constructive feedback. Implementing consistent follow-up processes is another crucial aspect of maintaining accountability. Regular check-ins and progress reviews ensure that expectations are met and provide opportunities to address any obstacles or challenges that may arise. These processes keep accountability at the forefront, reinforcing its importance and ensuring it remains a core component of the team's culture.

Accountability Reflection Exercise:

- **Reflect on a Recent Success:** Identify a recent project or task where you took ownership and achieved your goals. Consider what strategies and actions contributed to this success and how to apply them to future endeavors. The Accountability Reflection Exercise is a tool to help you reflect on your past achievements and identify the strategies that worked for you.

- **Identify Areas for Improvement:** Consider a situation where accountability could have been stronger. Reflect on the factors that contributed to any challenges and consider how you can implement strategies to enhance accountability in similar situations moving forward.

Accountability and ownership are the cornerstones of a high-performing team. Organizations can create an environment of trust, engagement, and excellence by fostering a culture where individuals are empowered to take responsibility for their actions. HR professionals have a role in this process as they implement strategies and policies that promote accountability and ownership. Teams can navigate challenges and achieve remarkable success through their commitment to continuous improvement.

4.2 Reinforcing Values through Consistent Actions

Consider a workplace where every action, from top leadership decisions to daily operations, aligns seamlessly with core organizational values. This alignment is a powerful driver of trust and accountability. When your team sees that values aren't just words on a poster but woven into everyday tasks' fabric, an environment of trust flourishes. This trust reduces uncertainty, making team members feel more secure and at ease. Employees can predict behaviors and decisions, reducing uncertainty and fostering a sense of security. This alignment shows that the organization stands by its principles, making it easier for team members to commit wholeheartedly to their roles. In such an environment, values become a guiding light, providing clarity and direction for everyone involved.

Implementing structured, value-driven decision-making frameworks can effectively ensure that actions consistently reflect organizational values. These frameworks serve as a checklist, or guide, reminding teams to consider core values at every decision point. For instance, if collaboration is valuable, decisions about project management tools or team structures should prioritize enhancing teamwork. A value-driven decision-making framework is a structured approach that ensures the organization's core values are considered and upheld in every choice.

Another practical step is organizing regular value alignment workshops. These sessions provide a platform for discussing how values translate into daily actions and assessing whether current practices align with stated values. By engaging team members in open discussions, these workshops reinforce the importance of values and encourage everyone to contribute to maintaining alignment.

The impact of values on trust and accountability cannot be overstated. When actions align with values, team alignment and cohesion increase. Team members are more likely to work together effectively when they share a common understanding of overarching goals. This shared understanding encourages a sense of unity, as the same principles guide everyone. Moreover, an organization that consistently acts according to its values enhances its reputation. Stakeholders, including clients, partners, and the public, see a company that practices what it preaches, boosting trust and credibility.

This enhanced reputation can open doors to new opportunities and partnerships, further driving organizational success. However, maintaining value consistency comes with its challenges. One significant obstacle is overcoming value-action gaps, where stated values must align with actual behaviors. These gaps can erode trust as employees and stakeholders question the organization's integrity. To address this, regularly assess and recalibrate actions to ensure they reflect values. This assessment can be done by revisiting policies, procedures, and practices to identify areas where alignment is lacking, then making necessary adjustments.

Another challenge is ensuring that leadership models "value-driven" behavior. Leaders set the tone for the organization, and their actions must embody the values they espouse. If leaders do not consistently demonstrate the company's values, it sends mixed signals that can undermine trust and accountability. Continuous training and development programs can help leaders internalize and exemplify these values for their employees.

Value-driven models refer to business approaches or frameworks in which decisions and strategies are centered on delivering the most value to customers, stakeholders, or society rather than focusing solely on profit. In value-driven models, the emphasis is on creating long-term value by aligning with customers' core needs and preferences and fostering ethical, sustainable, and impactful business practices.

Key elements of value-driven models include:

1. **Customer-centricity**: Prioritizing customer needs and delivering exceptional value through products or services that solve their problems or enhance their lives.

2. **Sustainability and Ethics**: Focusing on long-term impact, incorporating sustainable practices, ethical supply chains, and a commitment to social responsibility.

3. **Innovation**: Continuously improving products, services, or processes to create more value for customers or stakeholders.

4. **Stakeholder Consideration**: The wellbeing of all stakeholders, including employees, partners, the community, and the environment, must be considered.

5. **Quality and Experience**: Enhancing the customer experience and offering high-quality, value-rich solutions, often leading to brand loyalty and trust.

For example, companies like Patagonia or TOMS Shoes adopt value-driven models by aligning their business strategies with sustainability, ethical production, and giving back to communities, creating value for customers and broader society.

4.3 Empathy and Trust: Bridging Cultural Gaps

Empathy bridges cultural divides in today's diverse workplaces, building trust and understanding among team members from different backgrounds. The magic of empathy lies in its ability to help us perceive the world through someone else's eyes. In culturally diverse teams, this understanding is vital. It means recognizing and appreciating cultural nuances that shape how individuals communicate, solve problems, and collaborate. Empathy allows team members to move beyond stereotypes and assumptions, fostering a genuine connection that acknowledges and respects differences.

Practicing empathy requires intentional effort, but the rewards are significant. One effective method for cultivating empathy is through active listening workshops. These workshops focus on honing the skill of truly listening—not just hearing words but understanding the emotions and intentions behind them. These workshops help dismantle communication barriers and build stronger relationships by encouraging team members to engage fully in conversations. Another approach is cross-cultural training sessions. These sessions provide insights into various cultural norms and values, equipping team members with the knowledge to work through diverse interactions thoughtfully. Participants learn to recognize cultural cues and adapt their communication styles, reducing misunderstandings and fostering a more inclusive environment.

The benefits of empathy in diverse teams extend beyond individual relationships. Empathy leads to improved collaboration across cultural boundaries. Common goals aid in team members being willing to share ideas and work together toward common goals. This openness enhances creativity and problem-solving, as diverse perspectives contribute to more innovative solutions. When individuals perceive their distinctive viewpoints as valued, they are more inclined to engage actively and contribute meaningfully to the team's success. The resulting synergy creates a dynamic where diversity is not just tolerated but celebrated as a source of strength and inspiration.

Real-world examples highlight the transformative power of empathy in bridging cultural gaps. Consider a multinational company implementing an empathy-driven trust-building initiative across its global offices. The company recognized that cultural differences were causing misunderstandings and hindering collaboration. To address this, they organized empathy workshops and cross-cultural training for employees at all levels. The initiative focused on fostering open dialogue and understanding, encouraging employees to share their cultural experiences and perspectives. As a result, trust among team members increased significantly, leading to more effective collaboration and enhanced innovation. The company saw tangible improvements in project outcomes and employee satisfaction, demonstrating that empathy is a powerful tool for building cohesive and successful teams.

Through empathy, diverse teams can move beyond mere coexistence and into thriving collaboration. It is a skill that brings out the best in individuals and teams, turning potential cultural challenges into opportunities for growth and innovation. As organizations embrace diversity, empathy will be increasingly important in fostering mutual trust and ensuring every team member feels valued and included.

4.4 Trust-building Strategies for Hybrid Teams

Teams working remotely and in-office encounter distinct trust challenges. The most obvious hurdle is the difference in visibility. On-site team members often interact more face-to-face, naturally fostering connections and trust. Meanwhile, remote colleagues may feel left out of these organic exchanges, leading to a sense of isolation. This discrepancy can result in a divide where remote workers have a lesser sense of connection to the team's pulse and dynamics. Perceived communication barriers further complicate matters.

Without the benefit of impromptu hallway conversations or immediate feedback, misunderstandings can fester, and the nuances of communication often get lost in digital translation. For hybrid teams to thrive, address these challenges head-on. One effective way to build trust in hybrid teams is through structured activities that promote cohesion and understanding. Virtual team retreats are an excellent option.

These retreats create opportunities for team members to interact outside their usual work environment, fostering a sense of camaraderie and unity. During these retreats, team-building exercises and discussions help engage employees with one another and allow them to connect personally. This is the same as part of the goal of business trips: meeting others in person to work through concerns or complete a planning project. Cross-functional project collaborations also play a key role in trust-building. Working together on various projects aids team members in valuing each other's strengths and fostering trust. These projects encourage open communication and shared goals, creating a sense of collective responsibility and achievement.

Using technology is another effective strategy for boosting trust in hybrid settings. Collaboration platforms like Slack or Microsoft Teams provide a virtual space for communication, sharing updates, and collaborating in real-time. These tools help replicate the immediacy of in-office interactions, ensuring remote employees remain engaged and informed. For a more immersive experience, have virtual meetings where you can see each other "face-to-face" through Zoom or other meeting platforms. We have observed offices where off-site or remote workers are logged into Zoom all day and on the screen, so if you need to speak with them, you walk in to see them and talk live. VR technology can simulate face-to-face interactions, allowing participants to engage more naturally and intuitively.

Leadership plays an indispensable role in fostering trust within hybrid teams. Through their actions and communication, leaders set the tone for trust and reliability. Consistent and transparent communication from leaders is important. By regularly updating the team on goals, progress, and changes, leaders can ensure everyone is on the same page, regardless of location.

This transparency helps to build confidence and trust, as team members are informed and valued. These clear expectations and goals articulate what is expected of each team member and how their contributions align with the team's objective, fostering a sense of purpose and accountability. This clarity eliminates ambiguity and helps team members focus on achieving shared goals.

In hybrid environments, a foundation of trust is more important than ever. Hybrid teams can overcome challenges by addressing visibility differences, leveraging technology, and embracing collaborative activities. Leaders' role in this process is pivotal, as they guide the team with transparency and clarity. As we transition to the next chapter, we'll explore innovative strategies for enhancing team dynamics and collaboration, building on the trust and accountability established in hybrid teams.

Chapter Five

Enhancing Team Dynamics and Collaboration

"Individually, we are one drop. Together, we are an ocean." — Ryunosuke Satoro, Japanese author

T hink about a bustling kitchen in a renowned restaurant. Chefs and staff work harmoniously, seamlessly adapting to each other's moves, ensuring that each dish reaches the customer perfectly timed and expertly prepared. This fluidity mirrors the agile methodology, a concept designed not for culinary arts but for team operations, promoting flexibility and responsiveness.

5.1 Agility and Adaptability

Agile working principles have revolutionized how teams operate, originating in software development but extending far beyond. At its heart, agility is about iterative progress, where small, manageable tasks lead to substantial achievements over time. It emphasizes collaboration, ensuring that every team member's input shapes the outcome. Adaptability is its cornerstone, allowing teams to pivot swiftly in response to changes, much like chefs adjusting a recipe on the fly.

The benefits of adopting agile methods are profound, reshaping team dynamics and boosting productivity. Teams find that decision-making accelerates, as agility encourages swift, informed choices rather than lengthy, drawn-out deliberations. This speed is crucial in environments where time is a valuable commodity. Moreover, agility enhances adaptability, teaching teams to view change as an ally rather than a foe. This mindset shift allows teams to embrace disruptions, transforming potential setbacks into opportunities for innovation and growth. Agile work's iterative nature ensures continuous feedback, helping teams refine processes and outcomes efficiently. These elements create a dynamic where teams meet—and often exceed—their goals, driven by a shared vision and collective effort.

Transitioning to agile working methods requires strategic planning and commitment. Regular, stand-up meetings become a staple, providing a daily platform for team members to share progress, address challenges, and realign their efforts. These meetings are brief but powerful, ensuring everyone is informed and engaged. Sprint planning and retrospectives are integral, setting clear objectives for short work periods and reviewing outcomes to identify improvements. These cycles promote a rhythm of continuous learning and adaptation, which is essential for agile success.

Physical and digital Kanban boards are visual tools to track tasks and workflows, offering transparency and accountability. Kanban boards help teams stay focused and motivated by making progress visible to all. More importantly, they reinforce a culture of trust and collaboration, a key intangible benefit of agility.

Kanban is a workflow management method to help teams and organizations visualize work, improve efficiency, and ensure smooth project execution. It originated from lean manufacturing practices in Japan, specifically Toyota's production system, but has since been widely adapted for software development, project management, and other areas.

Kanban's core idea is to visualize work, limit ongoing tasks, and optimize task flow. It is particularly popular in agile and lean project management but can be applied to various industries and team sizes.

Here's how it works:

Elements of Kanban

- **Visualizing Workflow:** Kanban uses a board (physical or digital) divided into columns that represent different stages of a process, such as "To Do", "In Progress", and "Done". Each task is represented by a card that moves from left to right as it progresses through the workflow.

- **Limiting Work in Progress (WIP):** One of the principles of Kanban is to set limits on the number of tasks that can be in progress at once. This helps teams focus on completing tasks rather than starting too many things simultaneously, reducing bottlenecks and improving efficiency.

- **Focusing on Flow:** The goal is to keep tasks moving smoothly through each stage without unnecessary delays. By identifying where work gets stuck, teams can adjust to improve the overall flow and delivery speed.

- **Continuous Improvement:** Kanban encourages continuous monitoring and improvement. By regularly reviewing the board and analyzing performance, teams can identify areas to optimize and improve their workflow.

Benefits of Kanban

- **Flexibility:** Kanban doesn't impose strict planning processes and allows work to be reprioritized dynamically.

- **Focus on Delivery:** It emphasizes delivering work consistently and quickly, reducing the cycle time from task initiation to completion.

- **Transparency:** Kanban boards' visual nature makes it easy for everyone involved to see the status of tasks and understand potential roadblocks.

Example:

A digital marketing team using a Kanban board to manage a campaign creates cards for tasks like "Design banner ad", "Write blog post", and "Review social media plan". Each task moves across columns like "Backlog", "In Progress", "Review", and "Completed" as the team works on them. By limiting the number of tasks in the "In Progress" column, the team avoids overloading any one person and ensures that tasks are completed before new ones are started.

Consider the story of a software company that embraced agility to revitalize its operations. Initially bogged down by rigid hierarchies and lengthy approval processes, the company needed help keeping up with competitors. By adopting agile practices, it transformed into a fast-moving, innovative powerhouse. Stand-up meetings replaced endless email threads, fostering direct communication and rapid problem-solving. Sprint planning ensured that projects stayed on track, with teams regularly reviewing and adjusting their strategies. The result greatly increased productivity and morale, as employees were empowered and engaged, prepared to embrace new challenges and propel the company forward.

Similarly, a marketing department found success by integrating agile principles. Streamlined workflow and collaboration under agile methods accelerated campaign development. These transformations highlight how embracing agile can lead to remarkable improvements, making teams more resilient and innovative in the face of change. The speed and efficiency of agile methods were instrumental in this success, demonstrating their practical benefits in a specific context.

Agility Self-assessment Checklist:

- **Assess Team Readiness:** Evaluate your team's current practices and openness to change. Identify areas where agile principles can be integrated to enhance flexibility and responsiveness.

- **Implement Stand-up Meetings:** Introduce daily briefings to discuss progress and challenges. Encourage open communication and collaboration, ensuring everyone is aligned.

- **Utilize Kanban Boards:** Set up visual task boards to track workflows and progress. Use these tools to promote transparency and accountability within the team.

- **Conduct Retrospectives:** Schedule regular review sessions to reflect on outcomes and identify areas for improvement, creating a culture of continuous learning and adaptation.

5.2 Cross-functional Teams: Collaboration Across Boundaries

The essence of cross-functional teams consists of individuals from various departments or areas of expertise working toward a common goal. They break down silos, fostering collaboration that goes beyond the confines of a single discipline. In this setup, the marketing guru works alongside the tech whiz and the finance expert, each contributing unique insights to the project. The significance of such teams lies in their ability to drive innovation and problem-solving, leveraging the diverse skills and perspectives each member brings to the table.

Successful cross-functional teams' characteristics vary with their members. However, they all share a few key traits. Firstly, they possess a shared vision that aligns with the organization's goals. This vision is a guiding star, ensuring that all efforts are focused and coherent. Secondly, successful teams thrive on open communication, where each member is valued and heard, fostering a sense of inclusion and mutual respect. This openness allows ideas to flow freely and solutions to emerge organically. Lastly, these teams are adaptable, ready to pivot and adjust as new challenges and opportunities arise. This flexibility ensures that they remain dynamic and responsive, capable of navigating the complexities of the modern workplace.

Cross-functional collaboration offers numerous benefits that can transform an organization. One of the most significant is the boost in creativity and innovation it brings. By bringing together individuals with different backgrounds and expertise, these teams can approach problems from multiple angles, uncovering innovative solutions that might have otherwise remained obscured. Diverse thoughts drive creativity, sparking fresh ideas. Additionally, cross-functional teams benefit from a broader range of skills and expertise. This diversity allows them to tackle complex problems more effectively, drawing on a wealth of knowledge and experience that spans various disciplines. The result is a more holistic approach to problem-solving, where a comprehensive understanding of the issue informs solutions.

Setting up successful cross-functional teams necessitates meticulous planning and execution. One of the first steps is to set clear goals and objectives. This clarity ensures that all team members are aligned and working toward the same outcome. Defining roles and responsibilities is essential, providing a framework that guides interactions and collaborations. Open communication channels, such as regular formal and informal meetings, allow team members to share updates, voice concerns, and collaborate on solutions. These interactions build trust and cohesion, strengthening the team's ability to work effectively. Implementing dedicated team liaisons can further improve communication, connecting various departments and ensuring that information flows smoothly and efficiently.

Consider the example of a retail company that harnessed the power of cross-functional teams for product development. Facing stiff competition and a rapidly changing market, the company brought together marketing, design, supply chain, and technology experts to develop a new product line. This collaboration allowed the team to integrate insights from each area, resulting in a product that was innovative, practical, and aligned with customer needs. The successful project led to increased sales and a stronger market position. Similarly, a tech firm faced a challenge integrating new technologies into its product lineup. By forming a cross-functional team that included engineers, product managers, and customer service representatives, the company was able to develop a seamless integration strategy that enhanced user experience and satisfaction. These examples illustrate the transformative potential of cross-functional collaboration, unlocking new levels of innovation and success.

5.3 Creating a Feedback-rich Culture

In any thriving organization, the heartbeat of progress is a feedback-rich culture. Continuous feedback is a pillar of effective teamwork, driving team dynamics and individual performance to new heights. When feedback flows freely, it shapes a culture of constant improvement, where each member is committed to learning and evolving. This environment encourages open and honest communication, fostering trust among colleagues. It dismantles barriers, allowing for transparent exchanges where ideas are shared without fear of judgment. The outcome is a vibrant workplace where innovation thrives, as team members are empowered to contribute and collaborate.

Regular feedback is a powerful catalyst for personal and professional growth within teams. It acts as a mirror, reflecting one's strengths and highlighting areas needing development. This insight is invaluable, as it guides individuals on their path to improvement. Employees who receive consistent feedback are more engaged as they understand their impact and contributions. This engagement translates into increased motivation, with team members striving to achieve and surpass their goals. By identifying strengths, feedback allows individuals to leverage their talents effectively, enhancing overall team performance. Simultaneously, addressing areas for development ensures that skills are continuously honed and refined, fostering a culture of excellence.

Fostering a feedback-rich environment requires deliberate action and commitment. Implementing regular one-on-one feedback sessions provides a dedicated space for open dialogue, where employees can discuss their progress, challenges, and aspirations. This personalized approach ensures that feedback is tailored and relevant, enhancing its impact. Encouraging peer-to-peer feedback opportunities further enriches the feedback culture. Teams benefit from diverse perspectives and collaborative problem-solving by creating platforms for colleagues to share insights. This peer-driven approach promotes a sense of camaraderie and mutual support, strengthening team bonds. Additionally, creating an anonymous feedback platform can be highly effective. This tool allows team members to provide honest feedback without fear of repercussions, ensuring that all voices are heard and valued.

Consider the case of a consulting firm that transformed its operations through a feedback-driven development approach. Understanding the potential of feedback to stimulate innovation, the organization incorporated feedback mechanisms into its core processes. Regular feedback sessions became a staple, where consultants and managers engaged in constructive discussions about project outcomes and individual performance. This open dialogue nurtured a culture of trust and accountability, where everyone took responsibility for the firm's success. As a result, the firm experienced significant improvements in project delivery and client satisfaction, as teams were more aligned and motivated.

Similarly, a creative agency implemented peer feedback programs to enhance collaboration and creativity. The agency created an environment of mutual respect and continuous learning by encouraging team members to share feedback on each other's work. This approach led to a surge in creative output, as teams were inspired to experiment and innovate without fear of failure.

5.4 Leveraging Emotional Intelligence for Team Success

Picture a team functioning like a well-oiled machine, where members communicate seamlessly and resolve conflicts with minimal friction. Emotional intelligence

(EI) plays a pivotal role in creating such dynamics. As discussed in Chapter 3, EI involves the ability to recognize and manage one's emotions while also understanding and influencing the feelings of others. In a team setting, emotional awareness helps individuals to identify and communicate their emotions, creating an atmosphere where everyone is listened to. This awareness goes hand-in-hand with emotional regulation, which enables team members to maintain composure and respond thoughtfully, even in high-pressure situations. By honing these skills, teams can enhance communication, ensuring that interactions are productive and respectful.

Moreover, empathy and social skills are integral components of EI that significantly impact team interactions. Empathy involves stepping into another's shoes and grasping their perspectives and emotions. It builds trust and rapport, encouraging open dialogue and collaboration. When team members practice empathy, they create a culture of support and understanding where diverse viewpoints are valued. Social skills, however, encompass navigating social complexities, resolving conflicts, and building solid relationships. A team with high EI excels in these areas, fostering a harmonious work environment where matters are addressed constructively and relationships are nurtured. This foundation of trust and mutual respect is invaluable for effective collaboration and innovation.

The benefits of high EI in teams extend beyond improved communication; they enhance problem-solving and conflict resolution. Teams with high EI tackle challenges with agility, leveraging their emotional insights to find creative solutions. They approach problems with a collaborative mindset, drawing on the strengths and perspectives of each member. This inclusive problem-solving process leads to innovative outcomes that might otherwise remain unexplored. Additionally, high EI teams excel in conflict management. They address disagreements with empathy and understanding, focusing on resolution rather than blame. This approach efficiently resolves conflicts and strengthens relationships, as team members are respected and valued.

Building EI within teams necessitates purposeful effort and practice. One effective strategy is conducting EI training workshops and seminars. These sessions provide a structured framework for team members to enhance their emotional awareness, empathy, and social skills. Through interactive activities and discussions, participants gain insights into their emotional responses and learn practical management techniques. Role-playing exercises deepen empathy by allowing team members to explore different perspectives and experiences. This hands-on approach nurtures empathy and understanding, building stronger connections within the team. Self-reflection and mindfulness practices also play a crucial role in developing EI. Mindfulness enhances focus and clarity, enabling individuals to respond thoughtfully rather than impulsively.

Real-world examples illustrate the transformative impact of EI on team dynamics. Consider a healthcare team that embraced EI to improve collaboration and patient care. Facing high-stress situations daily, the team integrated EI training into their routine. By developing emotional awareness and empathy, team members enhanced communication with patients and each other. This approach improved patient outcomes and strengthened team cohesion and morale.

Similarly, a customer service team leveraged EI to enhance customer interactions. By honing their empathy and social skills, representatives were better equipped to understand and address customer needs, leading to higher satisfaction and loyalty. These examples demonstrate that EI is a theoretical and practical tool that can elevate team performance and dynamics.

Chapter Six

Cultural Transformation and Change Management

"The world hates change, yet it is the only thing that has brought change." - Charles Kettering

Consider a company that prides itself on innovation and employee empowerment. However, beneath the surface, a growing disconnect between its stated values and the actual experiences of its workforce is evident. This disconnect, known as cultural misalignment, is more than a divergence between an organization's proclaimed values and internal culture. This disconnect leads to confusion, frustration, and other problems that hinder the organization's ability to thrive.

6.1 Cultural Misalignment

One clear indicator of misalignment is high turnover rates. When employees believe their values clash with those of the organization, they often leave to seek better alignment elsewhere. Another sign is employee disengagement. Disengaged employees may remain with the company, but their lack of enthusiasm and commitment can erode productivity and morale. When departmental goals clash, it indicates a lack of alignment, with various teams working toward objectives that do not match the organization's mission. This lack of cohesion can lead to inefficiencies and internal tensions, further exacerbating the problem.

Identifying cultural misalignment requires a thoughtful approach. Several diagnostic tools and assessments can help uncover these discrepancies. Cultural audits and surveys offer valuable insights into employee perceptions and experiences, shedding light on areas where alignment falters. These surveys can ask employees to rate how well the company's actions align with its stated values. Employee focus groups provide open discussions where employees can freely voice their insights and concerns. These group sessions reveal patterns and themes that might not emerge through surveys alone. Leadership interviews are another essential tool, offering a top-down perspective on cultural alignment. Organizations can identify gaps between leaders' intentions and employees' daily realities by engaging leaders in candid discussions.

The impact of cultural misalignment on organizational performance and morale can be profound. When employees perceive a disconnect between stated values and actual practices, trust in leadership can erode. This erosion hampers productivity and stifles innovation, as employees may need more time to engage in their work or share new ideas fully. Internal conflicts often arise, fueled by competing interests and unclear priorities. These conflicts drain energy and resources, diverting attention from strategic objectives. The consequences of misalignment ripple across the organization, affecting employee satisfaction and the company's ability to attract and retain top talent.

Cultural Alignment Checklist:

- **Conduct a Cultural Audit:** Initiate a comprehensive assessment of your organization's culture through surveys and focus groups to identify discrepancies between stated values and actual practices.

- **Analyze Turnover Rates:** Investigate patterns in employee exits to determine if misalignment is a contributing factor.

- **Facilitate Leadership Interviews:** Engage leaders in discussions to understand their perspectives on cultural alignment and areas for improvement.

It is essential to tackle cultural misalignment to cultivate a healthy and productive work environment. By understanding its signs and impacts and employing practical diagnostic tools, organizations can realign their culture with their core values, paving the way for sustainable success.

6.2 The Change Agent's Toolkit: A Step-by-Step Guide

Change agents are the backbone of transformation in any organization seeking to evolve. These individuals drive change, guiding teams through the process of transformation. Their role is not just important; it's indispensable. It requires a specific set of skills and characteristics. Resilience tops the list. Change frequently encounters resistance, and resilient change agents remain steadfast, adapting to setbacks and persevering through challenges. Change agents must pivot strategies and approaches as organizational landscapes shift, responding to new information and feedback. Strong communication skills are essential, too. Effective change agents articulate the vision and rally support, so everyone understands their role in the transformation process.

Successfully implementing cultural change requires a structured approach. The first step is to set clear objectives and goals. This clarity in purpose aligns the team, ensuring everyone understands what success looks like and why change is necessary. Once objectives are set, engaging stakeholders becomes essential. Building relationships and securing buy-in from those affected by the shift supports a sense of ownership and commitment. With stakeholder support, initiatives can continue. Crafting a comprehensive change plan progresses, providing a roadmap for the transformation. This plan outlines necessary tasks, timelines, resources, and responsibilities, providing a clear path forward.

Change management software can streamline planning and execution. These digital tools offer platforms for tracking progress, managing tasks, and ensuring accountability. They offer visibility into the process, allowing teams to monitor milestones and adjust strategies. Communication platforms are equally important, helping engage stakeholders effectively. Tools like Slack or Microsoft Teams foster ongoing dialogue, enabling real-time updates and feedback. These platforms break down communication barriers, ensuring all voices are heard and everyone stays informed of developments.

Ongoing support and training are the lifeline of successful change management. Continuous support reinforces the transformation efforts, providing encouragement and resources to those navigating change. Workshops and training sessions offer opportunities to build new skills and knowledge, helping individuals adapt to new roles and responsibilities. Sessions must engage and interact with participant needs. Continuous feedback mechanisms are essential, too, allowing for adjustments and refinements throughout the process. Regular feedback provides valuable insights into what's working and not, enabling teams to make informed decisions and course corrections.

Change Agent Self-assessment:

- **Evaluate Resilience:** Reflect on past experiences where you faced challenges. How did you respond? Consider ways to enhance your resilience in future change initiatives.

- **Strengthen Communication Skills:** Identify areas where your communication could improve. Practice articulating complex ideas clearly and concisely to different audiences.

- **Enhance Adaptability:** Think about situations where flexibility was required. How can you become more adaptable in navigating change?

- **Utilize Change Management Tools:** Familiarize yourself with digital tools to support your change management efforts. Experiment with software and platforms to find what works best for your team.

The role of a change agent is challenging and rewarding in the dynamic environment of organizational change. Change agents can effectively lead teams through transformative initiatives by embracing the steps outlined here and utilizing the right tools and resources.

6.3 Overcoming Resistance with Empathetic Leadership

Change can be unsettling. It challenges the status quo and often prompts resistance, a natural human reaction. When employees face cultural shifts, several sources of resistance typically arise. Most fear is of the unknown. Employees may worry about the future and need clarification about how changes affect their roles and responsibilities, leading to anxiety, which can manifest in hesitance or outright opposition to change. Alongside this, the loss of routine or comfort presents another barrier. Established processes and familiar habits offer a sense of security and predictability. Change disrupts this comfort zone, compelling employees to adapt to new working methods, which can be daunting. Concerns about job security also loom large. Employees may question their place in the new organizational structure, wondering if their skills will remain relevant or their positions might be at risk. If addressed, these concerns can help any change initiative's success.

Empathy is key in addressing these fears and easing the transition process. Empathetic leadership involves understanding and sharing your team's feelings and creating a supportive environment where concerns are heard and validated. By listening to employee concerns, leaders demonstrate that they value their team members' perspectives.

Example of Active Listening in Business:

Scenario: A team member expresses concerns about a project deadline.

Team Member: "I'm worried we won't be able to meet the deadline due to the additional tasks that were added."

Active Listener: "I understand you're concerned about the added workload affecting the timeline. To make sure we're aligned, do you think the current deadline seems unrealistic with the new tasks?"

Team Member: "Exactly."

Active Listener: "Got it. Let's discuss how we can reprioritize or delegate tasks to stay on track or if we need to negotiate an extension."

This response shows active listening but pivots quickly toward finding solutions, which is critical in a business environment.

Business Context Emphasis:

- **Efficiency:** Active listening in business emphasizes actionable outcomes and maintaining focus.

- **Clarity:** Ensuring everyone clearly understands the points raised to prevent miscommunication.

- **Professionalism:** While still being empathetic, it's essential to maintain a professional demeanor that is aligned with business etiquette.

Overall, active listening in business is about balancing empathy and understanding with a focus on problem-solving, efficiency, and achieving business goals.

When leaders acknowledge and validate these emotions, employees are respected and understood, which decreases resistance and promotes a sense of inclusion. Empathy acts as a bridge, connecting leaders with their teams on a human level and building trust and openness essential for navigating change.

One-on-one meetings provide a dedicated space for individual conversations, allowing leaders to address personal concerns, offer tailored support, and allow the employee the safety of a private conversation. Open forums, on the other hand, facilitate collective dialogue, where team members can share their experiences and learn from each other. These forums promote transparency and inclusivity, ensuring that all voices are heard. Creating safe spaces for feedback is another vital strategy. Leaders should create an environment where employees are comfortable sharing their opinions without fear of judgment or repercussions. By encouraging open and honest feedback, leaders can gain valuable insights into the challenges and concerns of their team, allowing them to be proactive and effective.

Real-world examples highlight the success of empathetic leadership in overcoming resistance. Consider a healthcare organization undergoing a significant digital transformation. Initially, there was substantial pushback from staff accustomed to traditional methods. The leadership team noted this resistance and carried out a series of empathy-driven initiatives. They organized regular one-on-one meetings with staff to discuss individual concerns and provide reassurance. Open forums allowed employees to voice their challenges and collaborate on solutions. The leadership also established a feedback system, ensuring staff input was considered in decision-making.

As a result, resistance diminished, and the organization experienced a smoother transition to the new digital systems. Staff engagement and morale improved significantly, illustrating the power of empathy in driving successful change.

6.4 Measuring Success in Cultural Transformation

Analyzing the effectiveness of cultural transformation requires a discerning eye and a clear set of metrics. Employee engagement scores serve as a fundamental indicator. They reveal the depth of connection and commitment employees experience toward their work and the organization. High engagement levels often signal a thriving culture, while low scores may suggest areas needing attention. Turnover rates and retention metrics offer additional insights. A decrease in turnover and an increase in retention typically reflect a positive cultural shift where employees find value and satisfaction in their roles. These metrics clearly show how well cultural changes resonate with the workforce, offering a tangible measure of progress.

Qualitative and quantitative methods are essential in capturing the nuances of cultural transformation. Employee surveys and feedback forms are valuable tools for gathering quantitative data. They allow organizations to track changes in attitudes and satisfaction over time, providing a snapshot of the current cultural climate. These surveys should encourage honest responses, ensuring the data accurately reflects employee sentiments. On the qualitative side, observing cultural behaviors and practices offers a deeper understanding of how changes manifest in daily operations. Observations can uncover subtleties that numbers alone might miss, such as shifts in team dynamics or communication patterns. By combining these methods, organizations can build a comprehensive view of their cultural evolution.

Several successful frameworks have been developed to track and measure cultural transformation effectively. Balanced scorecards, for example, integrate financial and non-financial metrics to provide a holistic view of organizational performance. Organizations can align their strategic goals with cultural objectives by incorporating cultural metrics into these scorecards. Cultural dashboards are another innovative tool. They visually display key cultural indicators, making it easy for leaders to monitor progress and identify trends. These dashboards can be customized to track specific metrics relevant to the organization's goals, offering a real-time snapshot of cultural health. Both balanced scorecards and cultural dashboards provide structured approaches to measuring cultural transformation, ensuring that changes are implemented and sustained.

Continuous improvement is the backbone of lasting cultural change. Regular review meetings allow teams to reflect on progress, celebrate successes, and identify areas for further development. These meetings should be collaborative, encouraging open dialogue and diverse perspectives. Iterative feedback loops are equally important. They create a cycle of ongoing evaluation and adjustment, ensuring that cultural initiatives remain relevant and effective. Organizations can make informed decisions and refine their strategies by soliciting continuous feedback from employees and stakeholders. This commitment to continuous improvement strengthens a culture of adaptability and resilience, positioning the organization for long-term success.

Cultural Transformation Metrics Checklist:

- **Employee Engagement Surveys:** Implement regular surveys to track changes in engagement and satisfaction levels.

- **Turnover and Retention Analysis:** Monitor turnover rates to assess the impact of cultural changes on employee retention.

- **Cultural Behavior Observations:** Conduct regular observations to capture qualitative data on cultural dynamics.

- **Balanced Scorecards and Dashboards:** These tools align cultural metrics with strategic goals.

In cultural transformation, measuring success is as important as the transformation itself. Organizations can employ key metrics and frameworks to ensure their cultural initiatives are effective and enduring.

Tools

Implementing effective cultural transformation within an organization requires the use of specialized tools and services to monitor and assess various metrics. Below are some highly rated (at the time of this writing) companies and tools that can assist in the areas you've outlined:

1. Employee Engagement Surveys:

- **Qualtrics XM:** Offers comprehensive employee engagement surveys with advanced analytics to gauge satisfaction and engagement levels.

- **SurveyMonkey:** Provides customizable survey templates to collect employee feedback efficiently.

- **CultureMonkey:** Specializes in employee engagement surveys with actionable insights to drive cultural change.

2. Turnover and Retention Analysis:

- **Workday:** An HR platform that includes analytics for monitoring turnover rates and retention metrics.

- **BambooHR:** Offers tools to track employee turnover and retention statistics, aiding in understanding the impact of cultural initiatives.

3. Cultural Behavior Observations:

- **Glint:** Provides real-time employee feedback and sentiment analysis to observe cultural behaviors.

- **15Five:** Facilitates continuous feedback and performance reviews, offering insights into cultural dynamics.

4. Balanced Scorecards and Dashboards:

- **ClearPoint Strategy:** A balanced scorecard software that aligns cultural metrics with strategic goals through customizable dashboards.

- **BSC Designer:** Offers tools to create and manage balanced scorecards, integrating cultural transformation metrics.

- **Corporater:** Provides balanced scorecard software with features to monitor and manage performance metrics related to cultural transformation.

Do-It-Yourself (DIY) Tools

These tools provide software or platforms that allow organizations to independently measure, analyze, and track cultural transformation metrics:

1. **Qualtrics XM**-Users create and deploy their own surveys and dash-

boards.
Support: Offers customer support and resources for implementation.

2. **SurveyMonkey**-Customizable survey templates allow users to design and analyze their own surveys.
   Support: Extensive knowledge base and customer support are available.

3. **CultureMonkey**-Provides tools to set up and run employee engagement surveys with actionable insights.
   Support: Offers built-in analytics and suggestions.

4. **BambooHR**-Users manage retention and turnover data via the platform's HR analytics tools.
   Support: Customer support is available for onboarding.

5. **ClearPoint Strategy**-Allows organizations to create and manage balanced scorecards and dashboards internally.
   Support: Offers training resources for using the platform effectively.

6. **BSC Designer**
   DIY: Enables users to design and implement balanced scorecards independently.
   Support: Tutorials and customer support are available.

7. **15Five**-Tools for continuous feedback and performance management are user-operated.
   Support: Provides templates, guides, and customer support.

Consultancy/Service-Based Options

These services often involve experts or consultants working with organizations to design and implement solutions:

1. **Glint (part of LinkedIn)**-While offering a user-friendly platform, Glint provides consulting and data-driven insights to guide organizations in their transformation.

2. **Corporater**-This is primarily a service-based solution where consul-

tants help align balanced scorecards with organizational goals.

3. **Workday-A**lthough Workday offers tools for HR analytics, it often involves onboarding services and consultancy to maximize its capabilities.

DIY vs. Consultancy

- **DIY Tools** are cost-effective, giving organizations control over their processes but requiring internal resources and expertise to use effectively.

- **Consultancy Options** offer professional guidance, reducing the internal workload but at a higher cost.

Make a Difference with Your Review

"The best way to find yourself is to lose yourself in the service of others." – Mahatma Gandhi

T hink about a workplace struggling to connect—teams divided, innovation stalled, and employees feeling uninspired. Now imagine that same workplace transformed: collaboration is buzzing, creativity is flourishing, and every person feels valued. What made the difference? Someone like you shared the knowledge to spark that transformation.

This is where you come in.

I have a question for you...

Would you help someone you've never met, even if you never got credit for it?

Who is this person, you ask? They're someone trying to turn a struggling organization into a thriving, modern workplace. Maybe they're a leader wanting to build a culture of trust and belonging. Or maybe they're someone just starting out, looking for guidance and hope.

They're someone like you.

Our Mission
The mission of *The Modern Workplace Culture Made Easy* is to make creating

a thriving workplace culture accessible to everyone. Everything I do stems from that mission. And the only way to make this happen is to reach...well...everyone.

This Is Where You Come In
Most people judge a book by its cover—and its reviews. That's why I'm asking for your help, on behalf of someone who might be sitting in an uninspired workplace right now, wondering where to start.

Your review could make a huge difference. It could help:

- One more manager find the tools to lead with empathy.

- One more team feel connected and valued.

- One more organization turn chaos into clarity.

Your review costs no money and less than 60 seconds to write, but it can change someone's workplace—and maybe even their life—forever.

How to Help
To get that "feel good" feeling and help for real, all you need to do is leave a review.

Simply scan the QR code below or visit this link to share your thoughts:

[https://www.amazon.com/review/review-your-purchases/?asin=BOOKASIN]

If you feel good about helping someone you'll never meet, welcome to the club. You're one of us.

Thank you from the bottom of my heart. Now, back to creating cultures where people thrive!

– Your biggest fan, Sage Lifestyle Press

P.S. Fun fact: When you give to others, you give value to yourself. If you know someone who needs this book, share it with them. You could be the catalyst for their next breakthrough.

Chapter Seven

Measuring and Sustaining Cultural Success

"Of the six critical elements of work fit, culture fit is the hardest to grasp. It is largely invisible, unwritten and unspoken, but paradoxically, it causes employees the greatest pain, dissatisfaction, frustration and failure to thrive." - Carrick and Dunaway

C onsider a dynamic tech startup brimming with the spirit of innovation with a team that is its fountain of ideas, yet there's a problem. Despite the buzz, staff turnover is high, and engagement is declining. The founders recognize that, while creativity is abundant, their workplace culture needs attention. They implemented a robust framework for measuring cultural success, understanding that what is measured can be managed. As they embarked on this process, they concentrated on key metrics that would unveil the true heartbeat of their organization.

7.1 Assessing Culture

Metrics for assessing cultural impact are akin to a health checkup for your organization. Employee satisfaction and engagement scores are key indicators. These scores offer insights into employees' perceptions about their work environment, roles, and relationships within the company. High satisfaction often correlates with lower turnover rates, meaning employees are content and less likely to leave. On the contrary, low scores can signal a need for immediate intervention. Retention metrics further complement this analysis, revealing employee longevity and loyalty trends. When high turnover becomes a pattern, it can disrupt continuity and drain resources. By closely monitoring these metrics, leaders can pinpoint areas for improvement and celebrate areas of strength, ensuring a healthy cultural climate.

A comprehensive approach to cultural measurement necessitates both quantitative and qualitative data. While numbers tell part of the story, personal insights provide depth and context. Surveys and interviews are invaluable tools for gathering qualitative data. You can uncover employees' genuine feelings about their work environment through thoughtfully-crafted questions. These conversations often reveal unspoken challenges and opportunities for growth. On the other hand, performance metrics offer a quantitative view. They measure productivity, efficiency, and other tangible outcomes that reflect the cultural ethos. Together, these data forms paint a comprehensive picture of your organizational culture, helping you align it with your goals and values.

Successful measurement tools are the backbone of any cultural assessment initiative. Cultural health dashboards are becoming increasingly popular, offering real-time insights into various cultural indicators. These visual tools allow leaders to track trends and make data-driven decisions quickly. Balanced scorecards, another effective tool, integrate cultural metrics with overall business objectives. They provide a holistic view of how culture influences and interacts with business outcomes.

The Organizational Culture Assessment Instrument (OCAI) is another noteworthy tool for measuring culture based on the **Competing Values Framework**. Each tool offers unique features, and selecting the right one depends on your organization's needs and goals. The key is to choose a tool that provides clarity and actionable insights, empowering you to make informed decisions.

OCAI (www.ocai-online.com)

The **OCAI** is widely used to help organizations assess and understand their corporate culture. Developed by professors Robert E. Quinn and Kim S. Cameron at the University of Michigan, it is based on the Competing Values Framework (CVF), which categorizes organizational cultures into four distinct types.

The Four Culture Types in the OCAI:

Clan Culture:

- Focuses on collaboration and employee engagement.

- It's a family-like work environment focusing on mentoring, nurturing, and building loyalty.

- Leadership is typically seen as supportive, and the organization values teamwork, consensus, and participation.

Adhocracy Culture:

- Emphasizes innovation, creativity, and risk-taking.

- Organizations with adhocracy cultures are dynamic, entrepreneurial, and willing to experiment.

- Leadership is visionary, and the company values flexibility and adaptability.

Market Culture:

- Results-oriented, with a focus on competition and achieving concrete goals.

- Success is defined by market share, profitability, and winning against competitors.

- Leadership tends to be hard-driving and focused on productivity and efficiency.

Hierarchy Culture:

- Based on structure, control, and efficiency.

- Organizations with a hierarchy culture prioritize formalized procedures, clear lines of authority, and consistency.

- Leadership typically coordinates and monitors, focusing on stability and reliability.

How the OCAI Works:

The OCAI uses a survey in which participants assess their organization's current and preferred culture. The survey consists of six key dimensions of organizational culture:

1. **Dominant characteristics** (e.g., collaborative, competitive)

2. **Organizational leadership** (e.g., mentoring, results-oriented)

3. **Management of employees** (e.g., teamwork, productivity)

4. **Organizational glue** (e.g., loyalty, achievement)

5. **Strategic emphases** (e.g., long-term development, market position)

6. **Criteria of success** (e.g., customer satisfaction, stability)

Participants distribute points across the four culture types based on how much each kind describes their organization in its current state and how they would prefer it to be. The results clearly show the organization's dominant culture and how it might need to shift to align with strategic goals.

Applications of the OCAI:

- **Cultural Change**: Helps organizations identify gaps between their current and desired culture, guiding cultural change initiatives.

- **Strategic Alignment**: Aligns culture with organizational strategy to ensure cultural values support business goals.

- **Leadership Development**: Helps leaders understand their organization's cultural dynamics and how their leadership style can impact organizational culture.

In summary, the OCAI is a diagnostic tool that provides insights into an organization's culture and helps leaders and teams make informed decisions about changes and improvements.

Leadership is a cornerstone in steering cultural measurement efforts. Leaders must set clear measurement objectives, defining their goals and why they are significant. These objectives steer the measurement process, ensuring it aligns with organizational priorities. Once data is collected, the communication of results and actions becomes pivotal. Transparency in sharing findings encourages trust and collective ownership of cultural initiatives. Leaders create a collaborative environment where everyone is invested in cultural success by involving employees in interpreting and responding to data. Effective communication of results also highlights areas of progress, reinforcing positive behaviors and motivating continuous improvement.

To bring these concepts to life, consider the following interactive element to guide your role in the cultural measurement process.

Checklist for Cultural Measurement:

- **Define Key Metrics:** Identify which aspects of culture you aim to measure, such as satisfaction, engagement, and retention.

- **Select Tools:** Choose appropriate tools like cultural health dashboards or balanced scorecards to track these metrics.

- **Gather Qualitative Insights:** Conduct surveys and interviews to capture personal employee experiences.

- **Align Objectives:** As a leader, your role in setting clear objectives for what you hope to achieve with cultural measurement is important. These objectives guide the measurement process, ensuring it aligns with organizational priorities.

- **Communicate Findings:** Share results transparently, highlighting successes and areas for improvement.

By diligently applying these practices, you can transform your organization's culture into a powerhouse of engagement and innovation.

7.2 Sustaining Change: The Role of Continuous Improvement

Continuous improvement is a concept that breathes life into organizational culture. It's an ongoing, iterative process where enhancements are consistently made, ensuring that the culture stays stable but also evolves with the changing needs and aspirations of the organization. This process is akin to fine-tuning an intricate machine, where each minor adjustment contributes to a smoother and more efficient operation. The role of continuous improvement in cultural initiatives is critical; it ensures that once changes are implemented, they remain relevant and effective over time. By embedding this mindset into the organization's fabric, a continuous environment is established where growth and development are ongoing, not just occasional.

There are several impactful strategies to embed continuous improvement into cultural practices. Regular review and feedback sessions stand out as a key tool. These sessions allow for ongoing dialogue, reflection, and the sharing of insights and experiences, fostering a culture of learning and adaptation. Such meetings help identify areas that need attention and celebrate successes, ensuring everyone remains aligned with the cultural objectives. Another strategy is establishing a culture of learning and adaptation, where employees are encouraged to seek new knowledge and embrace change. This can be facilitated by providing access to training programs and resources that promote skill development and innovation. Encouraging innovation and experimentation is equally important by setting up a space that fosters team members' confidence in taking calculated risks and exploring new ideas to nurture a culture that thrives on creativity and continuous improvement.

The benefits of committing to continuous improvement are manifold. For starters, it significantly enhances employee engagement and satisfaction. Employees are valued and motivated to contribute when feedback brings tangible changes and improvements. This engagement translates into greater organizational flexibility as the culture becomes more adaptable and responsive to external changes and challenges. A commitment to continuous improvement also builds cultural resilience in a world where change is the only constant; organizations that adapt quickly and effectively are more likely to thrive. This adaptability ensures that cultural initiatives remain relevant and impactful as the business landscape evolves.

Several organizations have successfully integrated continuous improvement into their culture, serving as shining examples of its potential impact. Take a logistics company, for instance, that embraced iterative cultural refinement. By regularly reviewing and adjusting their cultural practices, they streamlined operations, reduced employee turnover, and increased overall satisfaction. Their commitment to continuous improvement enhanced their internal culture and improved customer service and operational efficiency. In another example, a tech firm implemented continuous improvement strategies across its operations. By fostering a culture of innovation and learning, the firm could adapt swiftly to technological advancements and market shifts, maintaining its competitive edge and reputation for excellence.

Incorporating continuous improvement into your organizational culture is not just about making changes; it's about creating a mindset where growth, learning, and adaptation are ingrained in every aspect of the organization. This approach sustains cultural initiatives and ensures they remain dynamic and aligned with the ever-evolving needs of the business and its people. Continuous improvement becomes a catalyst for lasting success, driving both personal and organizational development.

Continuous improvement models like Kaizen, PDCA, Lean Management, and Agile Methodology encourage an organizational culture of openness, collaboration, and incremental changes. They promote an environment where employees are engaged in ongoing development and businesses are agile and adaptable to change. Implementing these models can drive long-term cultural transformation, aligning organizational behavior with strategic objectives and fostering a sustainable culture of growth and innovation.

7.3 Celebrating Successes and Learning from Failures

Working for a company that values and celebrates every success, regardless of size, is ideal. It's a place where achievements are noted and lauded with genuine enthusiasm. Celebrating cultural successes sends a powerful message to the organization: your hard work is valued, and your contributions matter. When achievements are acknowledged, morale soars. Employees are driven to continue excelling, understanding that their efforts produce tangible recognition. This positive reinforcement encourages the repetition of successful behaviors, creating a cycle of ongoing improvement and engagement. Celebrations aren't merely about the momentary joy they bring; they embed a sense of accomplishment and pride within the team, fostering a culture where excellence becomes the norm.

To effectively celebrate and recognize achievements, organizations can take several actionable steps. Hosting recognition events and ceremonies provides a formal platform to honor outstanding contributions. These events can range from small team gatherings to larger company-wide celebrations, depending on the scale of the achievement. Another impactful strategy involves disseminating success stories through internal communications. Whether it's an email newsletter, a dedicated bulletin board, or an internal social media platform, these stories highlight achievements and inspire others. By showcasing individual and team successes, organizations create a narrative of triumph and ambition, encouraging everyone to strive for similar recognition. Recognizing excellence sets a standard and encourages ambition.

While celebrating successes is vital, learning from failures is equally important. Failure, when viewed constructively, is a powerful teacher. It provides insight into what went wrong and how similar pitfalls can be avoided. Analyzing failures can drive cultural growth and resilience, transforming setbacks into opportunities for improvement. Conducting failure analysis workshops is an effective way to facilitate this process. In these sessions, teams can dissect what happened, identify contributing factors, and brainstorm solutions to prevent recurrence. Encouraging a no-blame culture for experimentation is critical here. Employees who know they can experiment without fear of reprimand become more willing to take risks and explore innovative solutions. Valuing learning from mistakes as much as success is a key aspect of this experimental culture.

Examples abound of organizations that have effectively balanced celebration and learning. Consider a healthcare organization that instituted lessons-learned sessions following each major project. These sessions became a cornerstone of their operations, openly discussing successes and failures. The organization found that learning from past experiences could fine-tune its processes, improving patient care and operational efficiency. Similarly, a retail chain adopted celebratory initiatives to boost employee morale and motivation. They fostered a competitive, yet supportive, environment by regularly recognizing top-performing stores and individuals. Employees were appreciative and empowered to innovate, recognizing that their successes and learning experiences were valued.

7.4 Adapting Culture in a Fast-changing World

Maintaining cultural relevance amidst rapid change is a formidable challenge in the ever-evolving business landscape. Organizations today confront a whirlwind of technological advancements and disruptions that can render even the most established cultural norms obsolete overnight. As new technologies emerge, they often alter how we work, communicate, and think. For instance, integrating artificial intelligence into routine operations demands new skills and a shift in mindset and values. This technological upheaval requires cultures to be reactive and proactively adaptive, ensuring they remain aligned with the latest digital realities.

Simultaneously, shifts in workforce demographics bring an additional layer of complexity to cultural adaptation. As generations with distinct values and expectations enter the workforce, cultures must evolve to accommodate diverse perspectives. Millennials and Generation Z, for example, prioritize inclusivity, flexibility, and a sense of purpose in their work. These shifts challenge organizations to rethink their cultural frameworks, ensuring they resonate with a younger, more diverse workforce. However, it is important to note that age is not the only factor in this demographic evolution.

Organizations must adopt strategies that ensure their cultures remain adaptable and relevant. Conducting regular cultural audits is a crucial first move. These audits provide a clear snapshot of a culture, highlighting strengths and areas for improvement. By regularly assessing cultural health, organizations can make informed decisions about where to focus their efforts. Involving employees in change initiatives is just as crucial. When team members are involved in shaping culture, they are more likely to embrace changes and contribute positively. This engagement develops a sense of ownership and accountability throughout teams and the company, thus driving collective cultural evolution. Additionally, aligning culture with changing market demands ensures that cultural initiatives support broader business objectives. As markets evolve, so must the cultural strategies that underpin them.

Leadership plays an instrumental role in driving cultural adaptation. Leaders must model adaptability and openness to change, setting the tone for the rest of the organization. This involves demonstrating a willingness to embrace new ideas, technologies, and practices and encouraging others to do the same. Leaders inspire confidence and trust by leading by example and motivating employees to contribute to cultural evolution. Employees need to be involved in cultural adaptation efforts. Employees given the freedom and resources to experiment and innovate become active agents of change, driving the culture forward.

Consider the example of a media company that successfully navigated cultural adaptation in a rapidly-changing environment. Faced with the digital transformation of their industry, the company embraced agile practices, allowing them to respond swiftly to new trends and technologies. By fostering a culture of experimentation and learning, they survived and thrived, becoming a leader in digital content delivery. In another case, a financial services firm embarked on a cultural evolution to align with shifting customer expectations and technological advancements. Engaging employees at all levels created a culture of continuous improvement and innovation, ensuring long-term success in a competitive market.

These examples illustrate that cultural adaptation is about responding to external changes and proactively shaping a resilient, dynamic, and aligned culture.

Chapter Eight

Navigating Hybrid and Remote Work

"Flexible work makes employees loyal."-Michelle Obama

P icture this: a vibrant office bustling with energy, where team members engage in spontaneous conversations, share ideas, and build camaraderie over coffee breaks. This same vitality can be captured in the digital realm, where physical distance no longer dampens engagement. This is the challenge and promise of remote work—a landscape where keeping employee engagement requires intentional strategies and innovative solutions.

8.1 Engagement Enhancement

Remote work has become the norm for many, presenting unique challenges in maintaining employee engagement. The absence of face-to-face interactions may result in feelings of isolation and disconnection. Without the casual interactions that occur naturally in an office setting, team members may feel excluded from the social fabric that binds a team together. Moreover, monitoring productivity can be tricky, as the traditional engagement markers, such as visible collaboration and input during meetings, are less apparent in a virtual environment. This new reality demands a rethink of keeping the remote workforce engaged and connected.

To counteract these challenges, implementing engagement-enhancing strategies becomes vital. Virtual coffee breaks offer a simple, yet effective, way to recreate the informal interactions that occur in an office. Creating time for team members to gather online, share stories, and foster personal connections can aid in bridging the gap caused by physical distance. Similarly, encouraging participation in team-building games facilitates a sense of community and belonging. These activities break the workday's monotony and strengthen team bonds, making collaboration more seamless. However, it's not just about the activities themselves. It's about the culture they create.

Setting up consistent recognition and reward systems can enhance morale and motivation. Acknowledging and appreciating team members' efforts, regardless of location, reinforces their value to the organization and encourages continued engagement. These strategies remind employees that their contributions are seen and valued, fostering a culture of appreciation.

Technology, particularly communication platforms like Slack and Zoom, is pivotal in enhancing remote engagement. These tools provide virtual spaces where team members can interact in real time, share updates, and brainstorm ideas. By leveraging these platforms, teams can replicate some of the dynamics in traditional office settings, ensuring remote employees remain engaged and informed. Virtual reality tools take this further, providing immersive experiences that bring remote teams together in shared digital environments. Consider joining a virtual brainstorm where the team experiences a sense of closeness despite the distance. This level of immersion can enhance engagement and create a strong sense of connection among team members.

Successful remote engagement strategies are not just theoretical concepts; they have been implemented effectively by various organizations. Consider the case of an IT firm that faced the challenge of maintaining engagement among its remote workforce. The firm created a strong sense of community and connection among its employees by introducing regular virtual coffee breaks and team-building activities. These initiatives encouraged open communication and collaboration, increasing productivity and job satisfaction. Similarly, the firm implemented a recognition program acknowledging employee achievements through virtual celebrations and awards. This emphasis on recognition and appreciation further reinforced the firm's culture of engagement and motivation. These success stories show remote work's potential with the correct strategies and tools.

Another example of successful remote engagement is the use of quarterly virtual town hall meetings by a global company. These meetings serve as a platform for leadership to communicate updates, share company goals, and recognize employee contributions. The organization advances a sense of belonging and purpose among its remote workforce by involving employees in its vision and achievements. These events also allow employees to ask questions and provide feedback, promoting transparency and open dialogue. Through these efforts, the company has maintained high levels of engagement and alignment despite the challenges of remote work.

Virtual Engagement Strategy Checklist:

- **Host Regular Virtual Coffee Breaks:** Schedule informal online gatherings for team members to connect and socialize.

- **Encourage Team-building Activities:** Organize virtual games and activities to foster camaraderie and teamwork.

- **Implement Recognition Programs:** Establish systems to acknowledge and reward employee achievements and contributions.

- **Leverage Engagement Platforms:** Use tools like Slack and Zoom to facilitate communication and collaboration.

- **Explore Virtual Reality Tools:** Consider incorporating VR for immersive team experiences and brainstorming sessions.

By implementing thoughtful strategies and leveraging technology, organizations can create vibrant, connected environments where employees are engaged and valued, regardless of where they are physically. Techniques and tools in this chapter can turn remote work challenges into opportunities for growth and innovation.

8.2 Inclusion and Belonging in Hybrid Models

In the modern workplace, the hybrid model blends remote and in-office work benefits, aiming to provide flexibility and balance. However, it also creates a challenge in fostering a sense of inclusion and belonging among employees. An inclusive environment is one where remote and in-office employees are on equal footing, each having the same resources and opportunities for growth. This balance requires intentionality. It demands a culture that respects and values each person's contributions, building an atmosphere where acceptance is the norm, not the exception. This becomes the backbone that supports collaboration, innovation, and satisfaction across diverse teams.

Achieving this inclusion has its challenges. Disparities in access to information can create gaps between physical- present employees and those working remotely. In-office staff may benefit from impromptu meetings or hallway conversations, leaving remote colleagues disconnected. This can result in remote workers perceiving themselves as sidelined, as if they are on the periphery rather than at the heart of the team. The challenge is to ensure seamless communication and that everyone is included in these informal exchanges. If not addressed, these barriers can lead to disengagement and a loss of cohesion, weakening the team's overall effectiveness.

To overcome these challenges, organizations must adopt deliberate strategies to promote inclusion. One practical approach is rotating meeting facilitators. By doing so, diverse voices are given a platform, ensuring that everyone has the chance to lead discussions and contribute ideas. This practice democratizes meetings and empowers employees by valuing their perspectives. Conducting regular inclusivity training sessions can further reinforce this culture. These sessions educate teams about the importance of inclusion, helping them understand and appreciate their colleagues' diverse backgrounds and experiences. They serve as a reminder that inclusivity is an ongoing commitment, not a one-time initiative.

Creating mentorship programs connecting remote and in-office employees can bridge the gap between working environments. These programs pair employees with mentors who guide and support them, regardless of location. Organizations can build relationships that transcend physical boundaries by leveraging technology, encouraging collaboration and personal growth. These mentorships, facilitated by technology, can provide remote workers with insights and advice they might otherwise miss, ensuring they remain engaged with and integrated into the company's culture.

Consider the example of a global consultancy firm that has embraced hybrid inclusion initiatives. This firm recognized the need for a cohesive approach that valued all employees equally. The firm has successfully established an environment where everyone is included and valued through the implementation of structured mentoring programs and rotating leadership in meetings. These efforts increase innovation and productivity, as diverse ideas are brought to the forefront. In another case, a tech company used inclusive team-building activities to bring remote and in-office staff together. By organizing virtual workshops and collaborative projects, they fostered a shared purpose and, thus, a more cohesive team.

Inclusion in hybrid work models is more than ensuring everyone has a seat at the table; it's about ensuring every voice is heard and valued. It's about creating a culture where diversity is accepted and celebrated, where each employee feels they belong. By addressing the challenges head-on and implementing thoughtful strategies, companies can create inclusive environments that thrive in the hybrid landscape.

8.3 Balancing Work-life Dynamics in Remote Settings

Remote work has redefined the boundaries of our daily lives, often blurring the line between personal and professional spaces. The flexibility that once seemed appealing can quickly become challenging when you cannot separate work tasks from home life. It's easy to check emails late or skip breaks to squeeze in more work. Setting boundaries becomes difficult, leading to a constant state of "being at work", even when you're supposed to be off the clock. This lack of separation can increase the risk of burnout as employees struggle to switch off and recharge. Remote work can also disrupt daily routines without the routine of a commute or the clear delineation of office hours, making it harder to maintain a healthy balance. The kitchen table might become a makeshift desk; before you know it, work seeps into every corner of your life. The continuous blend of work and personal time can reduce productivity and wellbeing.

Best Practices for Employees

- Creating a specific workspace at home plays a role in achieving a work-life balance. This designated area helps signal the start and end of the workday, creating a physical boundary between work and personal life. By keeping work confined to this space, you can mentally shift from "work mode" to "home mode", reducing stress and enhancing focus. Setting precise work hours and break times further supports this balance.

- Define when your workday begins and ends within these boundaries. Schedule regular breaks to stretch, have meals, or step outside for fresh air. These breaks punctuate the day, preventing fatigue and maintaining energy levels.

Leadership plays a vital role in supporting remote teams' work-life balance. Encouraging time off and mental health days conveys that wellbeing is a priority. Leaders should actively promote taking breaks and using vacation days to prevent burnout. Leaders set an example for their team by modeling healthy work-life balance behaviors. When leaders demonstrate a commitment to balance by unplugging after hours or taking downtime, it normalizes this behavior to others. This leadership approach supports individuals and a culture where balance is valued, leading to happier and more productive employees.

Many organizations have successfully implemented initiatives to support work-life balance in remote settings. A tech company known for its innovative culture introduced a flexible scheduling policy, allowing employees to tailor their work hours to fit their personal needs. This approach acknowledges that productivity only sometimes aligns with a traditional 9-to-5 schedule and empowers employees to work when they are most focused. As a result, employees report decreased stress and an increased sense of control over their time, resulting in higher job satisfaction and improved performance. Another example is a company that implemented a "no-meeting Friday" policy. Employees can focus on deep work or take care of personal commitments by designating one day a week free from meetings. This initiative has reduced meeting fatigue and increased productivity, as team members have uninterrupted time to concentrate on important tasks. These examples illustrate how thoughtful policies can support work-life balance, even in a remote environment.

8.4 Building Community Virtually

In remote work, belonging and community become beacons of stability and morale. Traditionally, office environments naturally foster interactions—casual chats, shared lunches, and spontaneous brainstorming sessions. These moments build camaraderie and trust—essential components for any thriving team. In a virtual setting, however, these interactions don't occur naturally. This makes the deliberate building of a virtual community beneficial and necessary. A strong virtual community boosts team cohesion by ensuring everyone is part of something larger than themselves. It weaves individuals into the organization's fabric, reducing feelings of isolation often accompanying remote work. When team members establish a connection, morale improves, and productivity follows suit.

Yet, crafting this virtual community has its challenges. The absence of physical presence means that team members miss out on non-verbal cues and impromptu conversations. This lack of interaction can make it challenging to build the kind of rapport that happens naturally in person. Moreover, time zone differences and varied schedules can create hurdles, making finding standard windows for meetings or social gatherings tough. These barriers can lead to disconnectedness, where team members become more like isolated contributors than integral parts of a cohesive unit. Finding solutions to these obstacles requires creativity and dedication to fostering a sense of belonging despite lacking physical presence.

Organizations can implement a range of strategies. Hosting regular virtual social events is an excellent starting point. These events can vary from informal catch-ups to themed gatherings or virtual happy hours. The goal is to provide spaces where team members can relax and connect on a personal level. Creating online interest groups and forums allows individuals to bond over shared interests outside of work tasks. Whether it's a book club, a fitness challenge, or a cooking group, these forums offer avenues for employees to engage and form meaningful connections. Encouraging peer recognition programs further strengthens these bonds. When team members acknowledge and celebrate each other's achievements, it creates a culture of appreciation and support. Recognition may involve a shoutout in a meeting or a dedicated newsletter space.

Examples of successful virtual community initiatives provide valuable insights into what works. A multinational company, for instance, has organized virtual cultural festivals that celebrate the diversity of its workforce. These festivals include interactive workshops, performances, and discussions that engage employees from various locations. The initiative highlights the rich tapestry of cultures within the organization. Another example is a remote startup that tackled the challenge of community-building through innovation challenges. The startup created a dynamic and engaged community by organizing competitions encouraging employees to collaborate and innovate. These challenges sparked creativity and fostered connections among team members who might not otherwise interact regularly.

Building a solid virtual community becomes integral to maintaining a positive and productive workplace culture as we embrace remote work. It requires intentionality, creativity, and a commitment to all team members. By fostering this sense of community, organizations can overcome distance barriers and create environments where employees thrive.

Chapter Nine

Diversity, Inclusion, and Belonging

"A diverse mix of voices leads to better discussions, decisions, and outcomes for everyone." – Sundar Pichai

P icture an office where every voice matters. Employees greet each other with genuine smiles, and meetings buzz with diverse perspectives that fuel creativity and innovation. These interactions are not just a vision; they are the reality of an inclusive workplace. In this kind of setting, respect, equity, and openness are exemplified, creating an environment where individuals are valued and supported.

9.1 Inclusivity

Respect, equity, and openness are the cornerstones of an inclusive workplace. It's not just about diversity for its sake but also about integrating it into the organization's fabric. This strategic imperative enhances innovation, attracts top talent, and boosts employee engagement. Inclusive workplaces consistently outperform their peers, underscoring the benefits of fostering diversity and inclusion.

Organizations must take deliberate steps to build such an environment. Creating inclusive policies and practices is crucial for establishing the tone. Work toward creating guidelines that promote fairness, such as equal pay for equal work and fair project placement. Encouraging diverse hiring practices ensures that talent pools are rich with varied skills and backgrounds. Implementing blind recruitment techniques can help minimize unconscious bias during the hiring process.

Additionally, creating Employee Resource Groups (ERGs) provides support networks for underrepresented groups, offering a platform for their voices and promoting a sense of belonging. These groups can drive initiatives that align with the organization's goals, fostering a more inclusive culture. Top-level buy-in is not just a formality but a reinforcement of the organization's commitment to inclusion, making it a core value rather than an afterthought. It's a call to action for leaders to take responsibility and drive the change toward a more inclusive workplace.

The impact of inclusivity on employee morale is profound. When employees are valued and included, job satisfaction naturally increases. They are motivated to contribute to the overall success of an organization. Turnover rates decrease, as employees are less likely to seek opportunities elsewhere. Individuals in a workplace with an inclusive environment that empowers them to 'show up' will, in turn, experience a sense of loyalty and dedication, resulting in increased engagement and long-term success for the organization. This positive atmosphere encourages creativity and collaboration, driving the organization forward. Moreover, a diverse and inclusive culture enhances the organization's reputation, attracting top talent and setting it apart as an employer of choice.

Several organizations have successfully fostered inclusivity, setting examples for others to follow. Consider a financial firm implementing a comprehensive inclusion program, integrating diversity into every aspect of its operations. By establishing clear diversity goals and accountability measures, the firm ensured that inclusivity was not just a buzzword but a measurable outcome. This commitment led to increased employee satisfaction and improved performance. Another example is a design company that embraced inclusivity-driven innovation. By creating diverse teams and encouraging cross-functional collaboration, the company harnessed various perspectives, resulting in groundbreaking designs that resonated with global audiences. These examples demonstrate that inclusivity is a moral obligation and a strategic advantage that drives success.

Inclusivity Checklist:

- **Develop Inclusive Policies:** Ensure equal pay and fair project placement.

- **Encourage Diverse Hiring:** Implement blind recruitment and diverse talent pools.

- **Create ERGs:** Support underrepresented groups with networks and initiatives.

- **Foster Leadership Support:** Secure top-level buy-in for inclusivity as a core value.

- **Assess Impact:** Measure inclusivity's effect on morale and performance regularly.

9.2 Celebrating the Competitive Advantage of Diversity

Diversity is a powerful catalyst for creativity and innovation in the vibrant tapestry of modern workplaces. When people from diverse backgrounds collaborate, they contribute perspectives and experiences that often result in innovative solutions. This diversity of thought fuels creativity and empowers teams to tackle problems with fresh insights that may, otherwise, remain unexplored. The broader range of diverse teams' skills and experiences enhances problem-solving capabilities, enabling organizations to handle complex challenges with agility and creativity. When innovation is essential to your business, embracing diversity is beneficial and necessary.

Diversity is also a strategic market differentiator. In today's global economy, organizations that leverage diverse teams can expand their market reach by understanding a broader view of customer needs. Diverse teams drive market expansion by tapping into new demographics and creating products or services that resonate with varied audiences. Diverse teams bring valuable cultural insights that enhance the understanding of customer behavior and preferences, enabling companies to customize their offerings in ways competitors might miss. This advantage in customer understanding can significantly elevate a company's position in competitive markets, distinguishing it as a leader in innovation and customer satisfaction.

Embracing and celebrating diversity requires deliberate effort and strategic initiatives. One practical step is hosting cultural appreciation events celebrating different backgrounds and traditions. These events foster a sense of belonging and educate employees on the richness of diverse cultures, promoting mutual respect and understanding. Implementing diversity training programs is another effective strategy. These programs give employees the knowledge and skills to manage diverse environments, enhancing their ability to collaborate effectively. It's equally important to showcase a variety of role models within the organization. By showcasing the accomplishments and contributions of individuals from diverse backgrounds, organizations can inspire others and emphasize the importance of diversity. This recognition boosts morale and encourages a culture of inclusion and aspiration.

Organizations that have successfully embraced diversity often see remarkable results. Consider a tech company that focuses on diversity-led innovation. By building cross-functional teams with members from diverse backgrounds, the company was able to develop products that appealed to a global audience. This approach not only expanded their market reach but also resulted in a significant increase in revenue. Similarly, a company in the consumer goods sector experienced market success through diverse product teams. By integrating cultural insights into their product development process, they crafted offerings that resonated deeply with customers worldwide. These examples underscore the transformative power of diversity as a competitive advantage, demonstrating that it can drive success on multiple fronts.

9.3 Overcoming Barriers to Inclusion

Creating an inclusive workplace may present multiple obstacles, with unconscious bias and stereotypes being some of the most challenging to overcome. Though often unintentional, these biases can shape decisions and interactions that exclude or marginalize some employees. They manifest in recruitment, promotions, and daily workplace dynamics, creating invisible barriers that prevent a genuinely inclusive environment. For example, a manager might unknowingly favor candidates with similar backgrounds, thus perpetuating a cycle of homogeneity. Stereotypes, on the other hand, can lead to assumptions about capabilities based on gender, race, or other characteristics, limiting opportunities for those who don't fit the mold. Additionally, inequitable access to opportunities is a significant barrier. These disparities can hinder an organization's growth and development of diverse talents, whether through unequal access to mentorship, training, or challenging projects.

Organizations must take deliberate action to dismantle these barriers. Implementing unconscious bias training is a vital first step. Such training programs raise awareness about biases and provide strategies to mitigate their impact. They encourage employees to recognize their biases and understand how they affect their decisions. Implementing mentorship and sponsorship programs is another effective strategy. These programs provide underrepresented employees with experienced mentors who can guide their career development and advocate for advancement. By creating pathways for growth, organizations can ensure that all employees have equal opportunities to succeed.

It is also essential to review and revise company policies for inclusivity and potential biases. Consider setting clear promotion criteria, ensuring diverse representation in decision-making bodies, and establishing transparent processes for conflict resolution.

Continuous assessment is vital to maintaining progress in inclusion efforts. Organizations should conduct regular inclusion audits. These audits provide a holistic view of the workplace culture, highlighting strengths and areas requiring attention. Gathering feedback through employee surveys is another essential tool. Surveys can reveal how employees perceive the organization's inclusivity initiatives, offering insights into their effectiveness and areas for growth. By actively listening to employee feedback, organizations can adopt strategies that better meet the needs of their workforce, ensuring that inclusion efforts remain relevant and impactful.

Several organizations have successfully overcome significant barriers to inclusion through innovative initiatives. Consider a media company that launched a successful bias reduction program. By integrating bias training into their onboarding process and establishing a task force to review and recommend changes to hiring practices, they significantly increased the diversity of their workforce. This proactive approach broke down existing barriers and fostered a culture of inclusivity and innovation. In another example, a manufacturing firm implemented equitable opportunity initiatives that provided equal access to training and advancement opportunities. The firm created a diverse talent pipeline by partnering with educational institutions and offering scholarships and internships to underrepresented groups. This commitment to equity enriched the talent pool and enhanced the firm's reputation as an inclusive employer.

9.4 The Role of Leadership in Promoting Diversity

Leadership plays a vital role in driving diversity and inclusion within any organization. It's not just about setting policies; it's about embodying the change you wish to see. Leaders who commit to diversity goals set the tone for an inclusive culture. Their commitment is evident in the strategies they employ and the behaviors they model. When leaders prioritize diversity, it sends a powerful message throughout the organization that these values are integral to success. This commitment is not a one-time statement but a continuous effort to integrate diversity into the core of the organizational fabric. Modeling inclusive behaviors is equally essential. Leaders who actively include diverse opinions in decision-making demonstrate that every voice matters. This workplace is where employees feel appreciated, respected, and motivated to deliver their best performance.

Promoting diversity requires actionable strategies that leaders can implement. One practical approach is setting diversity targets and accountability measures. By establishing clear goals, leaders can track progress and ensure that diversity initiatives are aspirational and achievable. These targets should be specific, measurable, and aligned with the organization's objectives. Another powerful strategy involves promoting employee networks that focus on diversity. These networks provide a platform for underrepresented groups. Leaders should allocate resources to support these networks, ensuring they have the necessary tools and support to thrive.

Leaders can also champion diversity by investing in initiatives promoting inclusion and equity. This investment might include funding diversity training programs, sponsoring events celebrating cultural heritage, or launching campaigns highlighting the achievements of diverse employees. By allocating resources to these efforts, leaders demonstrate their commitment to creating an inclusive workplace where everyone can succeed.

Diversity in leadership is transformative. When leadership teams are diverse, they bring many perspectives and experiences. This diversity enhances decision-making, as leaders can draw from a broader pool of insights and ideas. Diverse leadership teams are better equipped to understand and meet the needs of a diverse workforce and customer base. They can identify opportunities and challenges that might be overlooked by more homogenous groups, leading to more innovative solutions and strategies. It is essential to boost representation at all organizational levels to nurture a culture of inclusion. When employees see themselves reflected in leadership, it reinforces the message that diversity is valued. This representation inspires confidence and encourages employees from all backgrounds to aspire to leadership roles, creating a pipeline of diverse talent that strengthens the organization.

Several organizations have successfully leveraged leadership to promote diversity and inclusion. Consider a retail chain that underwent a leadership-led diversity transformation. By prioritizing diversity in their hiring and promotion processes, the company created a leadership team that reflected the diversity of their customer base. This transformation improved employee morale and enhanced the connection of the company with its customers. Another example is the implementation of executive mentorship programs aimed at enhancing diversity. These programs pair senior leaders with emerging talent from diverse backgrounds, providing mentorship and career development opportunities. This initiative has been instrumental in increasing diversity within leadership ranks and fostering a culture of inclusion and innovation. These examples demonstrate that when leaders actively champion diversity and inclusion, they pave the way for organizational success and resilience.

As we conclude this chapter, it's clear that leadership is the driving force behind diversity and inclusion efforts. Leaders can create a workplace where everyone thrives by setting clear goals, modeling inclusive behaviors, and empowering diverse voices. The next chapter will explore how organizational development and leadership practices intersect to foster a dynamic, agile workplace culture.

Chapter Ten

Addressing Pain Points and Challenges

"We need diversity of thought in the world to face the new challenges." – Tim Berners-Lee

A renowned architecture firm was at a crossroads in the heart of a bustling metropolis. The firm was celebrated for its innovative designs, yet internally, there was a growing rift between the values professed by leadership and those held by its employees. This disconnect manifested subtly—declining morale, increased turnover, and projects that no longer inspired the same passion. The leaders, recognizing the threat this posed to their legacy, embarked on a mission to realign the company's values with those of their talented team. Let's dive into the profound importance of aligning employee and organizational value—a critical, yet often overlooked, aspect of workplace culture that holds the power to transform an organization from within.

10.1 Aligning Values

Aligning personal and company values is a necessary and meaningful tool for fostering employee engagement and satisfaction. Employees experience a deeper connection to their work when individual values, such as integrity, compassion, and innovation, resonate with an organization's guiding principles. This alignment fuels motivation, as individuals see their roles as more than just jobs; they become avenues for personal expression and growth. Moreover, when values align, loyalty flourishes. Employees are more likely to channel their efforts into the company's success, resulting in reduced turnover and a cohesive workplace culture where collaboration and innovation thrive, when they feel the company's values are honorable. Employees sense a strong alignment of values that fosters a sense of belonging, ensuring they are valued and supported, thereby boosting productivity and engagement. This alignment benefits the organization and individuals, making work more meaningful and fulfilling.

However, signs of misalignment can be subtle and may manifest over time. Disengagement is a primary indicator, often reflected in employees' lack of enthusiasm and diminished commitment to projects and goals. When individuals feel that their values are not aligned with the organization's, they may become disinterested, viewing their work as a mere obligation rather than a passion. This disconnect often leads to frequent value-driven conflicts, where employees clash with leadership or peers over decisions that contradict their personal beliefs. Such conflicts can erode trust and create a toxic work environment, further exacerbating disengagement and turnover. Identifying these signs is crucial for intervening and aligning values to regain harmony and purpose within the organization.

To successfully attain value alignment, intentional strategies that encourage open dialogue and reflection are necessary. Conducting value workshops and discussions allows employees to express their values and understand the organization's core principles. These workshops promote transparency and collaboration, allowing employees to see where their values intersect with the company's. Incorporating values into performance evaluations is another practical approach. By assessing how well employees embody organizational values, leaders reinforce the importance of alignment and encourage continuous improvement. Open dialogue about organizational goals further supports this alignment, creating a shared vision that inspires and motivates employees to invest in the company's long-term success.

Other strategies, such as making a values-based recognition program or integrating values into the hiring process, can also effectively align employee and organizational values. When implemented thoughtfully, these strategies can bridge gaps and create a cohesive culture that resonates with all team members.

Real-world examples underscore the transformative power of value alignment. Consider an NGO that revolutionized its recruitment process by prioritizing value alignment. By seeking candidates whose personal values aligned with the organization's mission of social justice and equity, the workforce became deeply committed to its cause. This alignment increased employee satisfaction and engagement, as individuals saw their roles as extensions of their personal beliefs and aspirations. Similarly, a tech startup successfully integrated values-based leadership training into its organizational culture.

The startup fostered an environment where innovation and integrity were ideals and lived experiences by equipping leaders with the tools to embody and promote company values. These examples illustrate how value alignment can drive success, creating workplaces where employees are motivated, loyal, and united in purpose. However, it's important to note that implementing value alignment strategies can also present challenges, such as resistance to change or difficulty in measuring the impact of these strategies.

Value Alignment Exercise:

Reflect on your values and how they align with your organization's values. Consider the following questions:

- What are your core values, and how do they influence your work and interactions?

- How do your values align with your organization's, and where do they diverge?

- What steps can you take to foster alignment and enhance engagement and satisfaction?

Engage in this exercise to deepen your understanding of value alignment and its impact on your professional journey.

10.2 Tackling Low Employee Engagement

In many workplaces, low employee engagement quietly undermines productivity and morale. It can be challenging to pinpoint why employees seem disengaged, but several root causes often contribute to this issue. A significant factor is the need for recognition and appreciation. Motivation declines when employees perceive that their efforts go unnoticed and enthusiasm wanes. Everyone wants to know that their challenging work matters and contributes to the organization's success. This acknowledgment is necessary for employees to believe in their value, and its absence leads to disengagement. Another critical factor is the scarcity of growth opportunities. Employees need to see a path for advancement and development. Without clear avenues for skill enhancement and career progression, stagnation creates a sense of futility.

When your employees are engaged, they are also more productive, innovative, and committed to their roles. The impact is profound. They find their work satisfying, translating into better job performance and outcomes for the organization. Studies consistently show a direct correlation between engagement levels and job satisfaction. Employees who are engaged are more likely to stay with the company, which helps lower turnover rates and recruitment and training expenses. In contrast, disengaged employees often contribute to high turnover, which disrupts team dynamics and drains organizational resources. Maintaining engaged employees is essential for upholding a stable and thriving workforce.

Employee engagement requires purposeful strategies and initiatives to be implemented. Implementing recognition and reward programs can significantly enhance engagement by acknowledging employees' efforts and achievements. Such programs don't have to be elaborate; even simple gestures like verbal praise or small tokens of appreciation can make a difference. Creating opportunities for skill development is equally important. Offering training sessions, workshops, and mentorship programs helps employees build new skills and, thus, see a way to advance their careers. This investment in their growth shows that the organization values their development and is committed to their future.

However, one of the most important strategies is establishing clear communication channels. When you keep Employees informed and involved in decision-making, they are more likely to be engaged and dedicated to the organization's goals. By ensuring clear communication, organizations can make employees feel more informed, involved, and engaged in the company's mission and vision.

Real-world examples illustrate how effective engagement initiatives can transform an organization. Take, for instance, a hospitality group that implemented an e-employee recognition platform. This platform allowed managers to acknowledge and celebrate employees' achievements in real time, creating a culture of appreciation and motivation. As a result, the group saw a marked increase in employee satisfaction and retention and improved guest experiences. Another example is a tech company that introduced career growth workshops. These workshops gave employees the tools and resources to develop new skills and pursue career advancement. The initiative boosted employee engagement and enhanced the company's innovation and competitiveness in the industry.

Enacting these strategies within your organization can foster a culture of engagement where employees perceive value and motivation. Recognition, growth opportunities, and open communication are vital elements that contribute to a thriving workplace environment. By focusing on the fundamental reasons behind disengagement and implementing purposeful initiatives, a workplace can be established where employees are motivated to give their utmost and steer the organization toward triumph.

10.3 Strategies to Combat Burnout and Stress

Burnout has become all too familiar in the modern workplace, characterized by emotional exhaustion, depersonalization, and a decreased sense of personal accomplishment. It's physically and mentally draining. Employees experiencing burnout frequently describe a sense of detachment from their work and colleagues, as if they're merely having chronic fatigue, irritability, and a pervasive sense of inadequacy. When left unchecked, burnout can lead to more severe health issues, impacting not only the individual's wellbeing but also the overall health of the organization.

The effects of burnout on organizations are profound and cannot be ignored. Burnout leads to increased absenteeism as employees struggle to muster the energy or motivation to attend work. This absenteeism disrupts team dynamics and places additional stress on those who must cover for absent colleagues. Moreover, burnout contributes to high turnover rates, as employees seek relief from unsustainable work environments by leaving the company altogether. This turnover incurs significant recruitment and training costs and erodes team cohesion and continuity. Productivity takes a hit, too, as burnout saps the creativity and efficiency that drive innovation and success. Morale plummets, creating a ripple effect that affects everyone within the organization, leading to a toxic cycle of stress and disengagement.

Preventing and managing burnout requires a proactive approach, focusing on prevention and support. Implementing flexible work arrangements is an important step. When companies allow employees to have a say in managing their work schedules to better suit their personal needs, organizations can help reduce stress and prevent burnout. This flexibility empowers employees to balance work responsibilities with personal obligations, increasing job satisfaction and engagement. Encouraging regular breaks and time off is equally important. Employees must periodically recharge and disconnect from work to maintain mental and physical health. Organizations should promote a culture where taking breaks is normalized and supported, recognizing that well-rested employees are more productive and committed.

Another vital strategy is providing access to mental health resources. Organizations must prioritize mental health by offering counseling services, stress management workshops, and mental health days. These resources support employees in managing stress and show that the organization values their wellbeing. By promoting an environment where mental health is supported and not brushed under the rug, companies can break the stigma and encourage employees to seek help when needed.

Consider a finance firm that recognized the impact of burnout on its workforce and implemented comprehensive mental health support programs. By offering counseling services and stress management workshops, the firm was able to significantly reduce burnout levels, leading to improved employee satisfaction and retention. Employees reported a greater sense of support and value, leading to a more positive and productive work environment. Similarly, a healthcare organization introduced stress reduction workshops to address the unique challenges faced by its staff. These workshops provided employees with practical tools to manage stress and build resilience, helping to mitigate burnout and improve overall wellbeing.

Organizations that take proactive steps to combat burnout enhance employee wellbeing and strengthen their competitive advantage. By fostering a supportive culture prioritizing mental health, they create a workplace where employees are motivated and engaged to do their best work.

10.4 Addressing Toxic Work Environments

The atmosphere in a toxic workplace is often filled with tension and unease, where the air is thick with gossip and blame games. A need marks these environments for more support and recognition, which can result in employees being left isolated and undervalued. Gossip spreads like wildfire, creating a culture of mistrust and suspicion. People are more focused on covering their tracks than collaborating with colleagues. Blame games become the norm, where pointing fingers precede solving problems. Leadership support is rare in such settings, and complex work recognition is even rarer. This lack of acknowledgment and appreciation leads to a sense of futility and disengagement, eroding the foundation of a once-harmonious workplace.

Toxic environments take a heavy toll on employee morale and organizational success. When negativity permeates the workplace, job satisfaction plummets. Employees dread coming to work, and their engagement levels are in a nosedive. They begin to question their purpose and role within the organization, which can result in higher turnover as they look for healthier work environments elsewhere. This constant churn disrupts team dynamics and damages the organization's reputation. Potential hires become wary, and the company needs help attracting top talent. The cycle of toxicity continues, impacting productivity and innovation, as employees are too consumed by the negative atmosphere to focus on creativity or growth. The organization is in a downward spiral, where achieving long-term success seems increasingly challenging.

Transforming a toxic work environment demands deliberate and strategic steps. The clear definition of behavioral expectations is the initial step. Leaders must set the tone by defining acceptable behaviors and modeling them consistently, helping employees understand what is expected and reducing ambiguity, paving the way for a more respectful workplace. It is equally essential to prioritize open and respectful communication. This openness of trust and transparency creates a culture where ideas are shared freely and conflicts are addressed constructively. Implementing conflict resolution mechanisms is another essential strategy. Equip teams with the tools to work through disagreements and find common ground, e.g., training and workshops that provide techniques to resolve conflicts amicably, ensuring that differences of opinion do not escalate into toxic encounters.

Examples of successful cultural transformations illustrate the power of these strategies in action. Consider a retail company that undertook a cultural reset initiative. Understanding the negative outcomes of gossip and blame, the company established a series of workshops to promote teamwork and communication. Leadership took an active role in fostering a positive environment, celebrating successes, and encouraging collaboration. Over time, the toxic behaviors lessened, and employees began to sense renewed camaraderie.

Another example is a law firm that faced significant internal conflicts. The firm empowered its employees to address disagreements constructively by introducing conflict resolution training programs. These programs emphasized empathy and understanding, transforming the firm's culture from discord to mutual respect and cooperation.

When addressing toxicity, it's vital to recognize that change doesn't happen overnight. It's a continuous process that requires commitment and persistence from all organizational levels. Companies establish clear expectations, promote open communication, and implement conflict resolution mechanisms. These efforts enhance employee morale and engagement, laying the foundation for sustainable organizational success. As we move forward, it becomes clear that building a thriving work environment involves ongoing dedication and collaboration.

Results of Toxicity:

Employee Turnover

- **Cost of Turnover**: Toxic work cultures contribute to increased turnover, with the cost of replacing an employee estimated to be between 50% and 200% of their annual salary due to recruiting, onboarding, and lost productivity costs.

- **2019 SHRM Study**: According to a survey by the Society for Human Resource Management (SHRM), 58% of employees who quit a job due to workplace culture cited specific elements of workplace toxicity as the main reason for their departure.

- **Toxic Culture Drives Turnover**: A 2022 MIT Sloan Management Review report found that toxic workplace culture was 10.4 times more likely to contribute to turnover than compensation.

Employee Engagement

- **Disengagement Rates**: Toxicity in the workplace leads to a significant drop in employee engagement. A Gallup study reported that disengaged employees cost U.S. companies $450 to $550 billion annually due to lost productivity.

- **Impact on Motivation**: Employees working in toxic environments are likelier to disengage emotionally from work, resulting in lower productivity, decreased innovation, and reduced discretionary effort.

Employee Morale and Wellbeing

- **Negative Impact on Morale**: Toxic workplaces severely damage employee morale. A study by Randstad US found that 58% of workers have left or considered leaving a job due to negative office politics, poor management, or toxic workplace culture.

- **Mental Health Issues**: Toxic work environments also contribute to increased stress and mental health issues. The American Psychological Association (APA) reports that job stress costs U.S. businesses over $300 billion annually due to absenteeism, employee turnover, diminished productivity, and increased medical, legal, and insurance costs.

- **Bullying and Harassment**: A 2021 survey by the Workplace Bullying Institute found that 30% of employees in the U.S. experience bullying in the workplace, which leads to decreased morale and mental health issues such as anxiety and depression.

Team Performance and Collaboration

- **Reduced Teamwork**: Toxicity undermines collaboration and teamwork, often creating siloed, distrustful work environments. Harvard Business Review found that employees in toxic environments were less likely to share ideas, provide feedback, or work cooperatively, resulting in lower team performance.

- **Conflict and Resentment**: Toxic workplaces often fuel interpersonal conflict and resentment, further damaging collaboration and productivity. Employees may spend more time navigating personal conflicts than focusing on their work.

Productivity Loss

- **Lost Productivity**: Toxic workplace behaviors such as bullying, micromanagement, and discrimination lead to disengagement and absenteeism, severely impacting productivity. The Workplace Bullying Institute estimates that 60% of toxic behaviors go unreported, but they significantly hinder day-to-day operations, resulting in lower overall performance.

The statistics show that workplace toxicity leads to higher turnover, lower engagement, declining morale, mental health issues, and reduced team performance, significantly hindering an organization's productivity and financial success. Many companies are increasingly focusing on improving workplace culture, supporting employee wellbeing, and fostering a positive, respectful work environment to prevent these negative outcomes.

Chapter Eleven

Real-world Applications and Case Studies

"Empathy Is Note Only A Nice-To-Have But The Glue And Accelerant For Business Transformation In The Next Era Of Business."-Steve Payne

I magine a busy hospital where the pace is relentless, and the stakes are high. Amid this hectic environment, a healthcare company grappled with high turnover, low morale, and disengaged employees. Leaders realized that a significant shift was necessary to reverse these trends. They leveraged empathy as a powerful tool to create a culture where employees experienced appreciation and understanding. This chapter delves into how empathy, a powerful force, became the cornerstone of a thriving cultural shift within this organization, providing a roadmap for others seeking a more compassionate workplace.

11.1 A Case for Empathy

The journey began with a bold vision: to embed empathy into every facet of the organization's culture. Leaders initiated empathy training programs designed to help employees at all levels understand and appreciate each other's perspectives.

These programs included workshops, role-playing exercises, and reflective practices encouraging staff to engage with their colleagues' experiences.

The goal was to foster a culture where listening and understanding were prioritized, leading to more meaningful interactions and stronger relationships. Simultaneously, the company integrated empathy into its leadership models. Leaders were encouraged to adopt empathetic approaches, ensuring that their decisions and interactions reflected a deep understanding of their teams' needs. This shift required a change in leadership style, moving from authoritative models to more collaborative and inclusive ones. Leaders participated in regular empathy coaching sessions, where they learned to navigate difficult conversations with compassion and to seek input from their teams before making decisions.

This approach empowered employees and built trust and loyalty, as team members felt their voices were heard and valued. The organization was profoundly affected by these changes. Employee satisfaction scores improved significantly, reflecting the positive shift in workplace dynamics. Staff members reported greater engagement and motivation while working in an environment that recognized and valued their contributions. This increased engagement translated into tangible organizational benefits, including reduced turnover rates. As employees became more invested in their roles, they were less likely to seek opportunities elsewhere, providing the company with a stable and committed workforce.

The company also saw decreased absenteeism and increased productivity, further demonstrating the success of the cultural change. The lessons learned from this case study offer valuable insights for other organizations looking to implement empathy-driven cultural change. One of the key takeaways is the importance of leadership buy-in. For empathy to become ingrained in a company's culture, it must be championed from the top down. As the driving force, leaders must model empathetic behaviors and demonstrate a genuine commitment to understanding and supporting their teams. This creates a chain reaction throughout the organization, empowering employees to adopt similar behaviors and take responsibility for the culture they create. Another critical insight is the need for continuous reinforcement of empathy-focused initiatives.

Cultural change doesn't happen overnight, as it requires ongoing effort and a steadfast commitment to maintain momentum. This healthcare company regularly revisited its empathy training programs, updating them to address emerging challenges and ensuring that new employees received the same foundational training. By embedding empathy into the organization's fabric, the company demonstrated its commitment to sustaining its cultural transformation and continued reaping the benefits of a more engaged and satisfied workforce. Empathy-driven change goes beyond strategy; it's a commitment to fostering a workplace where everyone feels valued and understood.

Organizations prioritizing empathy can foster environments supporting collaboration, innovation, and long-term success. This case study serves as a testament to the power of empathy in transforming workplace culture, offering a blueprint that others can follow to create meaningful and lasting change.

Empathy Integration Checklist:

- **Leadership Commitment:** Ensure leaders model empathetic behaviors and actively promote a culture of understanding.

- **Empathy Training:** Implement comprehensive programs that include workshops on active listening, role-playing exercises to understand different perspectives, and reflective practices to encourage staff to engage with their colleagues' experiences.

- **Continuous Reinforcement:** Regularly update and revisit empathy initiatives to address new challenges and integrate new employees.

- Employee Feedback: Encourage open dialogue and seek employee input to refine empathy strategies and practices.

11.2 Lessons from Industry Disruptors

In the ever-evolving business landscape, industry disruptors are pioneers who redefine norms and set new standards. Traditional rules do not bind these companies; they thrive on agility, constantly adapting to changing markets and consumer needs. Their capacity to pivot swiftly and effectively is a defining factor in their success. Disruptors are agile because they recognize that complacency is the enemy of innovation. They invest heavily in understanding market trends and consumer behaviors, allowing them to anticipate shifts and adjust their strategies accordingly. This proactive approach keeps them ahead of the curve, enabling them to seize opportunities others might miss. Their commitment to breaking traditional norms is not just about challenging the status quo; it's about creating new paradigms that offer better solutions, improved experiences, and greater value.

Cultural strategies that foster an entrepreneurial mindset are at the heart of these disruptors' success. They nurture environments where employees are encouraged to think like entrepreneurs, taking ownership of their projects and embracing the freedom to innovate. This culture of ownership extends beyond mere responsibility; it instills a sense of pride and motivation, driving employees to explore new ideas without fear of failure. Another key strategy involves promoting a culture of experimentation and risk-taking. Disruptors understand that not every idea will succeed, but each attempt brings valuable lessons. Establishing a culture that motivates teams to push boundaries and explore new territories starts with creating a safe environment for experimentation and learning. This willingness to experiment fuels a cycle of continuous improvement and innovation as employees learn from their successes and setbacks.

The impact of these innovative cultural practices on business success is profound. Disruptors often expand into new markets, leveraging their agile approaches to tap into emerging opportunities. Their agility in adapting enables them to seize trends and meet customer demands, establishing themselves as industry leaders. This adaptability translates into increased market share and brand recognition. Customers gravitate toward companies that offer fresh, relevant solutions, and disruptors deliver just that. Their reputation for innovation and forward-thinking strategies attracts a loyal customer base, solidifying their dominance in the market. As a result, these companies achieve financial success and shape industry standards and expectations.

Consider the case of a streaming service that revolutionized the entertainment industry. This company redefined content consumption by prioritizing a culture of innovation, offering viewers unparalleled access to a vast library of films and series. Their willingness to challenge traditional distribution models set them apart from competitors, enabling them to capture a significant market share. Similarly, a fintech company embraced agile transformation, disrupting the financial services sector by providing cutting-edge solutions to age-old problems. Their focus on agility and customer-centricity allowed them to rapidly develop and deploy new products, gaining tech-savvy consumers' trust and loyalty. These examples illustrate how cultural innovation can propel companies to the forefront of their industries, setting them up for sustained growth and influence.

Industry disruptors teach us that success is not just about having a great product or service but cultivating a culture that supports innovation, agility, and risk-taking. By fostering an entrepreneurial mindset and embracing experimentation, these companies create environments where creativity thrives and boundaries are pushed. Their impact is felt not only in their financial achievements but also in their ability to shape industries and inspire others to follow suit. Through their cultural strategies, disruptors challenge us to rethink how we approach business and to embrace change as an opportunity for growth and transformation.

11.3 Real-world Challenges and Solutions

Organizations often face many challenges when attempting to transform their workplace culture. One of the most persistent obstacles is the natural resistance to change. Change can be unsettling, and employees might be skeptical about new initiatives, harboring fear of the unknown or doubting their efficacy. This skepticism is compounded when there's a disconnect between what leadership envisions and what employees value. For instance, a company's leadership might prioritize innovation and risk-taking, while employees may value stability and clear directives. Such misalignments can lead to friction, making it challenging to execute cultural shifts effectively. When leadership and employee values diverge, trust can erode, and engagement dwindles, creating a barrier to achieving cohesive organizational goals.

Many organizations have turned to strategic solutions that prioritize transparent communication and stakeholder engagement to handle these challenges. Clear communication channels enable employees to express concerns, ask questions, and stay engaged in the change process. When leaders openly discuss the rationale behind cultural shifts and invite feedback, they demystify the transformation process, reducing fear and fostering trust. In addition to communication, tailored training and development programs are crucial in aligning leadership and employee values. These programs aim to educate employees about the benefits of the new cultural direction and provide them with the skills necessary to succeed. Customized workshops and training sessions can bridge the gap between leaders and employees, fostering a sense of unity and shared purpose.

The outcomes of implementing these solutions are striking. Organizations emphasizing transparency and engagement see a marked increase in employee buy-in and participation. As employees feel more connected to the organization's goals, their motivation and commitment naturally rise. This heightened engagement leads to a stronger alignment between organizational objectives and employee actions. When employees understand and support the company's vision, their work becomes more purposeful, contributing to higher productivity and morale. Furthermore, aligning values between leadership and employees creates a harmonious work environment where collaboration and innovation flourish.

Leaders hosted town hall meetings and small group discussions, fostering a safe environment for employees to voice their concerns and share insights. Leaders facilitated town hall meetings and small group discussions, creating a safe space for employees to express their concerns and offer insights. This approach eased fears and generated valuable feedback, which was used to refine the transformation strategy. As a result, employees felt more invested in the process, leading to a successful cultural shift that increased efficiency and morale.

A retail giant provides another compelling case study. This organization needed to work on the misalignment between the leadership's vision and employee values, which led to high turnover rates and low engagement. The company fostered a more inclusive and supportive culture by implementing a comprehensive initiative that aligned leadership actions with employee values. Leaders participated in empathy-building workshops and actively sought employee input on key initiatives. These efforts bridged the value gap, improving employee morale and a renewed sense of purpose. The organization's commitment to aligning leadership and employee values reduced turnover and enhanced overall performance and customer satisfaction.

When navigating cultural transformations, organizations must recognize the importance of addressing resistance and value misalignment head-on. They can overcome these challenges by prioritizing transparent communication and tailored development programs, fostering a more cohesive and productive workplace. The examples of the manufacturing firm and retail giant highlight the potential for positive change when organizations commit to aligning leadership and employee values, ultimately creating a culture where everyone thrives.

11.4 Scaling Culture: From Startup to Enterprise

Shifting a company's culture from a small startup to a large enterprise brings essential challenges. Maintaining a consistent and evolving culture becomes vital for sustaining innovation and agility as organizations grow. Culture acts as the backbone that supports a company's identity, guiding its values, behaviors, and decision-making processes. In the fast-paced world of startups, this culture often develops organically, driven by the passion and vision of a small team. However, as a company expands, particularly across multiple locations, the risk of cultural dilution increases. With careful nurturing, the core values that once defined the organization can become cohesive, leading to clarity and disengagement among employees. Thus, ensuring cultural consistency across locations and departments is essential for fostering a unified and motivated workforce.

Companies must establish a scalable cultural framework to scale and adapt to growth while preserving core values. This involves creating a set of guiding principles and practices that serve as a foundation for the entire organization. These principles should be clear, transferable, and flexible enough to accommodate different teams' and regions' unique needs. Technology plays a pivotal role in maintaining cultural connections as companies expand. Digital tools such as collaborative platforms, virtual town halls, and internal social networks can help bridge geographical gaps, enabling employees to engage with the company's culture regardless of location. These tools promote communication, collaboration, and the sharing of cultural narratives, ensuring that all employees are connected to the larger organizational community.

The impact of a strong, scalable culture on organizational success cannot be overstated. A cohesive culture enhances employee retention and attraction, as individuals are drawn to organizations with clear values and a supportive environment. Employees who resonate with the company's culture are likelier to remain loyal, reducing turnover rates and associated costs. Additionally, a well-defined culture builds organizational resilience and adaptability. It provides a stable framework within which innovation can flourish, allowing the company to respond effectively to market changes and challenges. This adaptability is a key competitive advantage, enabling businesses to overcome uncertainties and seize new opportunities.

Consider the case of a tech startup that successfully scaled its culture as it grew into a global enterprise. Initially known for its innovative spirit and collaborative ethos, the company faced the challenge of maintaining these values as it expanded into new markets. The company preserved its core values by implementing a scalable cultural framework centered around creativity and teamwork. Digital platforms facilitated cross-border communication, allowing teams to share ideas and collaborate seamlessly. This approach not only preserved the company's cultural identity but also strengthened its position as a leader in innovation.

Another example is a global corporation that undertook a deliberate cultural integration strategy during rapid growth. Upon realizing the importance of cultural alignment, the company developed a detailed cultural playbook that delineated its values, expectations, and practices. This playbook became a reference for all employees, ensuring consistency in behavior and decision-making. The company also invested in leadership development programs to instill cultural values at all levels, empowering leaders to act as cultural ambassadors. As a result, the organization achieved remarkable cohesion and engagement, driving sustained success in diverse markets.

Scaling culture is an ongoing process that demands continuous commitment and adaptability rather than a one-time effort. By establishing a robust cultural framework and leveraging technology to maintain connections, companies can ensure their culture thrives as they grow. A strong culture supports organizational success and inspires employees to contribute their best, creating a dynamic and resilient workplace. In the next chapter, we will explore how these cultural foundations can be leveraged to address the evolving challenges of the modern workplace, ensuring that organizations remain competitive and forward-thinking.

Chapter Twelve

The Future of Workplace Culture

"A company's culture is the foundation for future innovation. An entrepreneur's job is to build the foundation."-Brain Chesky

P icture yourself in a city square on a bright morning. The air is filled with the low rumble of conversations and the aroma of freshly-brewed coffee. People no longer follow the same old office routine. Instead, they head to co-working spaces, cafes, or even their living rooms. This scene captures the essence of how work has evolved.

12.1 Emerging Trends Shaping the Future of Workplace Culture

The landscape of workplace culture is shifting, driven by trends reshaping how we think about work. These changes influence our work locations, methods, and reasons. We must understand the trends shaping our future at this crossroads.

Flexible work arrangements have emerged as a dominant trend, with many orga-nizations embracing hybrid models. This shift empowers employees to balance professional and personal responsibilities more effectively, reducing burnout and increasing satisfaction. By offering flexibility, companies can tap into a diverse talent pool, no longer restricted by geographic boundaries. Employees oper-ate more efficiently when they work in the environments where they are most comfortable, supporting work-life balance and enhancing productivity. As more organizations adopt flexible policies, the traditional 9-to-5 is becoming a relic of the past, making way for a more adaptable and inclusive workplace culture.

Another significant trend is the increased focus on mental health and wellbeing. Organizations are recognizing that employee wellbeing is integral to performance and retention. Mental health initiatives like wellness programs and stress management workshops are becoming standard offerings. By prioritizing mental health, companies show they value their employees beyond their productivity, fostering a sense of trust and loyalty. This focus on wellbeing also drives a culture of openness, where employees feel safe discussing mental health challenges without stigma. As awareness of mental health grows, organizations that incorporate these practices into their culture will likely see increased engagement and lower turnover rates.

Sustainability and social responsibility are also taking center stage. Businesses are increasingly expected to demonstrate their commitment to the environment and social causes. This shift toward purpose-driven work environments reflects a broader societal demand for ethical business practices. Employees, particularly from younger generations, seek companies that share their values and make a positive impact on the world. By embedding sustainability into their culture, organizations meet these expectations and attract and retain talent that is passionate about making a difference. This alignment between business goals and ethical practices creates a powerful narrative that resonates with employees and consumers.

As these trends reshape the workplace, organizations must adapt their practices to remain competitive. Developing flexible work policies is an important first phase. Companies should offer remote work options, flexible hours, and support for work-life balance. Wellness and mental health programs can help create a supportive environment. Encouraging continuous learning ensures employees stay updated on skills and trends. Organizations can leverage online training and development platforms, fostering a lifelong learning culture. This approach enhances employee satisfaction and prepares them for future challenges, ensuring they remain agile in a rapidly changing world.

Reflection Section:

- **Reflect on Flexibility:** Consider how your current work setup supports or hinders your work-life balance. What changes would enhance your productivity and wellbeing?

- **Evaluate Mental Health Initiatives:** Assess your organization's approach to mental health. Are there programs or resources you find valuable? What additional support could be beneficial?

- **Sustainability Check:** Reflect on how your organization incorporates sustainability into its practices. How does this alignment with ethical values impact your motivation and purpose?

In this evolving landscape, continuous learning becomes essential. Promoting skill development and leveraging online learning platforms can help employees adjust to new roles and responsibilities. As organizations embrace these trends, they set the stage for a resilient workplace culture deeply connected to people's values and aspirations.

12.2 The Role of Technology in Shaping Culture

Technology is pivotal in reshaping workplace culture in rapidly evolving work environments. Step into an office where robots and algorithms handle routine tasks, allowing you and your colleagues to focus on creative and strategic endeavors. This transformation, driven by automation and artificial intelligence (AI), is altering the daily workflows within organizations. Automation handles repetitive tasks precisely, freeing humans to engage in more meaningful work. AI enhances decision-making by providing data-driven insights, enabling teams to work smarter and more efficiently. Yet, this shift also poses challenges, particularly in maintaining a balance between technological efficiency and human interaction.

Virtual and augmented reality (VR and AR) revolutionizes training and collaboration. Consider a team across continents coming together to brainstorm and innovate in a shared virtual space. These technologies create immersive learning experiences, breaking geographical barriers and fostering unity and community. They allow hands-on training without physical constraints, offering employees a more engaging way to develop skills. However, integrating these advanced tools requires careful implementation to avoid overwhelming users with excessive screen time, which can lead to digital burnout.

The benefits of technology integration are undeniable. One of the key benefits is the boost in efficiency and productivity. Automation streamlines processes, reducing errors and boosting output. VR and AR enhance learning and collaboration, making training sessions more interactive and effective. Despite these benefits, there are potential pitfalls. The rise of digital tools can lead to screen fatigue, affecting employee wellbeing and engagement. Over-reliance on technology may also erode interpersonal connections, undermining the very fabric of workplace culture.

Organizations must take deliberate steps to ensure technology enhances rather than detracts from workplace culture. Implementing digital wellness initiatives can mitigate the adverse effects of screen time. These programs encourage regular breaks, promote ergonomic practices, and support mental health. Balancing automation with human-centric practices is vital. While machines handle routine tasks, human creativity and empathy remain irreplaceable. Technology should augment human capabilities, not replace them. Even in virtual settings, encouraging face-to-face interactions helps maintain a sense of community and belonging, ensuring a balanced and healthy workplace culture.

Consider an e-commerce company that has effectively leveraged AI to revolutionize customer service. The company has allowed human agents to focus on complex customer interactions by employing chatbots for initial inquiries. This strategy boosts efficiency while enriching the customer experience, allowing employees to focus more on providing personalized service. Another example is a manufacturing firm that has integrated VR into its training programs. The firm simulates real-world scenarios and provides employees with practical experience in a safe environment. This innovative approach has reduced training costs and increased employee competence. Similarly, a global tech company has successfully implemented flexible work policies, allowing employees to work from anywhere, anytime. These examples illustrate how thoughtfully integrated technology and progressive workplace culture strategies can elevate workplace culture, driving performance and satisfaction.

As you navigate this technological landscape, it is critical to embrace innovation while remaining grounded in human values. By thoughtfully incorporating technology, you can build and sustain a culture that leverages the best of both worlds, empowering your organization to thrive in the face of change.

12.3 Preparing for Future Workplace Dynamics

The workplace of the future is rapidly evolving, influenced by a confluence of demographic shifts, the rise of unconventional work styles, and transformative changes in organizational structures. Imagine an office where colleagues span multiple generations, each bringing distinct perspectives and experiences. Today, workplaces are more diverse than ever, with baby boomers, Gen X, millennials, and Gen Z all working side by side. This multigenerational workforce presents both opportunities and challenges. The diversity of thought and experience leads to innovation but requires a nuanced approach to manage varying expectations and work styles. While younger employees may prioritize flexibility and purpose, seasoned professionals might value stability and structure. Balancing these diverse needs becomes crucial for organizations to foster a harmonious and productive environment.

Simultaneously, the gig economy has gained momentum, with freelance work becoming a preferred choice for many professionals. This shift challenges traditional employment models, prompting organizations to rethink their engagement with talent. Freelancers bring specialized skills and fresh perspectives, but managing a transient workforce requires adaptability and agility. Companies must establish systems that integrate gig workers seamlessly, ensuring they feel part of the team even though they may not be on-site daily. This need for flexibility extends to the organization, demanding structures that can pivot quickly in response to changing demands.

The dynamics of a diverse and multigenerational workforce offer a wealth of opportunities for innovation. Harnessing this group's diverse perspectives and experiences can spark creativity and drive progress forward. However, it also presents challenges in aligning different expectations and communication styles. Organizations need a culture that values and respects these differences, turning potential friction into opportunities for learning and growth. They should implement inclusive policies that cater to the needs of all employees, fostering an environment where everyone feels valued and heard. This inclusive approach boosts employee satisfaction and retention, positioning the organization as a top employer in a competitive job market.

Organizations must develop strategies that embrace diversity and flexibility to prepare for these future dynamics. Creating inclusive policies tailored to a diverse workforce is a foundational step. These policies should address equal opportunities, flexible work arrangements, and cultural sensitivity. Moreover, building agile and adaptable structures is essential. Organizations should avoid rigid hierarchies and adopt models promoting collaboration and innovation. This involves empowering employees to take initiative and make decisions, fostering a sense of ownership and accountability. By creating a culture of trust and empowerment, organizations can adapt to changes swiftly and effectively.

Consider a tech firm proactively embracing these future dynamics through strategic workforce planning initiatives. By analyzing workforce trends and anticipating future needs, the company has developed a talent strategy that aligns with its long-term goals. This includes investing in training programs to upskill employees and creating pathways for career advancement. The firm now has a resilient and adaptable workforce ready to tackle emerging challenges through these efforts. Another example is a consultancy that has adopted a flexible work model to accommodate the diverse needs of its staff. The consultancy has enhanced employee satisfaction and improved productivity and client satisfaction by offering remote work options and flexible hours. These examples illustrate the importance of forward-thinking approaches in preparing for the evolving workplace landscape.

12.4 Visionary Leadership: Inspiring the Next Generation

In the shifting landscape of today's workplace, visionary leadership stands as a beacon, guiding teams toward innovation and progress. Visionary leaders are forward-thinking, constantly scanning the horizon for new opportunities. They are not content with the status quo; instead, they challenge conventions and dare to imagine what could be. This contagious, innovative spirit inspires those around them to dream bigger and work harder. Visionary leaders also excel in motivating their teams through words and actions that align with a compelling vision. They create environments where creativity is nurtured and new ideas are welcomed, fostering a culture of continuous exploration and growth.

The influence of visionary leaders extends beyond immediate goals, as they play a key role in shaping future workplace culture. They provide a roadmap that aligns organizational efforts with larger aspirations by setting a clear and compelling vision for the future. This vision is a unified force, bringing together diverse talents and perspectives to achieve common objectives. Visionary leaders understand that innovation thrives in an atmosphere of creativity and openness, so they actively encourage experimentation and calculated risk-taking. They know that great ideas often come from unexpected places, and they cultivate a culture where everyone feels empowered to contribute their unique insights. This inclusive approach drives cultural evolution and ensures that the organization remains agile and adaptable in the face of change.

To develop visionary leadership within your organization, consider taking actionable steps that encourage these qualities. First, foster an environment where risk-taking is not only accepted but celebrated. Motivate your team to try new methods and embrace successes and failures as learning opportunities. This mindset promotes innovation and resilience, as employees feel safe to explore uncharted territory. Additionally, invest in mentorship and leadership development programs. Providing opportunities for emerging leaders to learn from experienced mentors can accelerate their growth and broaden their perspectives. These programs should focus on building strategic thinking, communication, and empathy skills, equipping future leaders with the tools to inspire and guide others.

Real-world examples of visionary leaders offer valuable insights into their transformative impact. Consider the case of a media mogul who embraced digital transformation at a time when many were skeptical. New technologies and platforms transformed the company under this leader's guidance, setting a fresh industry benchmark. Their forward-thinking approach inspired others to follow suit, leading to a wave of innovation that reshaped the media landscape. In another instance, an automotive CEO championed a shift toward sustainability, recognizing the growing demand for eco-friendly vehicles. By prioritizing research and development in electric and hybrid technologies, the CEO positioned the company as a leader in the green revolution. This commitment to innovation enhanced the company's reputation and attracted top talent eager to contribute to a meaningful cause. These examples highlight the power of visionary leadership to drive cultural transformation and inspire others to push boundaries.

As you reflect on the qualities of visionary leadership, consider how you can embody these traits within your organization. By fostering an environment that values innovation and creativity, you can inspire your team to reach new heights. Embrace the role of a visionary leader, setting a clear vision for the future and motivating others to join you on this exciting path. Together, you can shape a workplace culture that thrives on exploration and growth, paving the way for a brighter tomorrow.

Keeping the Game Alive

N ow that you've explored *The Modern Workplace Culture Made Easy* and gained the tools to build a thriving, inclusive workplace culture, it's time to share what you've learned and help others do the same.

Simply by leaving your honest opinion of this book on Amazon, you'll show other leaders, managers, and professionals where they can find the guidance they need to transform their workplaces. Your review can inspire others to take that first step toward creating better cultures where everyone thrives.

Thank you for your support. Workplace culture is kept alive and vibrant when we pass on what we've learned—and you're helping to do just that.

Conclusion

As we reach the end of our journey through modern workplace culture, let's take a moment to reflect on the insights and strategies we've explored together. This book has delved into the essential elements of building a thriving workplace, focusing on leadership improvement, organizational development, and embracing the dynamics of hybrid and remote work environments. We've highlighted actionable steps and evidence-based frameworks that can transform your organizational culture.

At the heart of these discussions lies the importance of fostering psychological safety. Establishing an environment where everyone can freely exchange ideas without concern for criticism is crucial for fostering a sense of safety. We've seen how integrating emotional intelligence into leadership enhances relationships and builds trust. Building trust and accountability isn't just a goal; it's a necessity for any successful organization. Improving diversity and inclusion raises workplace culture by aligning it with integrity, collaboration, and respect.

The lessons and strategies laid out in these pages are essential pathways for transforming your workplace culture. As you consider the insights shared, take them into your organization and become a proactive change agent. Cultivate a value-centric culture that thrives on continuous improvement and adapts to modern trends. You contribute to a more engaged, innovative, and resilient workplace with every step.

Leadership is crucial to driving this transformation. Adopt modern practices that promote vulnerability and authentic communication. As a leader, your behavior can set the tone for the entire organization. Modeling empathetic and accountable actions can inspire others to follow suit, driving positive cultural change.

I encourage you to reflect on your current workplace culture. Identify areas that need improvement and use the frameworks and case studies we've discussed as guides. Engage in empathy mapping and feedback loops to refine your approach continually. These tools are not just theoretical but practical guides for real change.

Gaining inspiration from actual instances shared in the book can be highly influential. We've shared stories of organizations that have successfully transformed their cultures. Let these examples motivate you to implement similar strategies in your context. The lessons learned from these case studies are invaluable.

Preparing for future workplace dynamics is important. Staying informed about emerging trends and effectively leveraging technology will help maintain a vibrant and adaptable culture. The workplace is ever-evolving, and being future-ready ensures you remain competitive and relevant.

As you embark on this cultural transformation quest, celebrate your progress. Recognize the successes and learn from any setbacks. Remember, this is an ongoing process that requires dedication and resilience.

Finally, we express gratitude for your commitment to improving workplace culture. Your efforts to create positive change will impact your organization and beyond. We support and encourage you as you take these next steps. Together, we can build workplaces that are not only successful but also fulfilling and enriching for everyone involved.

References

- *3 Real Cross-Functional Collaboration Examples| Miro Blog* https://m iro.com/blog/cross-functional-collaboration-examples/

- *6 Workplace Culture Trends for 2024 Every Company ...*https://www.greatplacetowork.com/resources/blog/6-work place-culture-trends-for-2024-every-company-should-watch

- *8 Tips for Building Transparency in the Workplace* https://www.better works.com/magazine/workplace-transparency-alignment-trust/

- *9 RemoteEmployee Engagement Strategies in2023*https://www.namanhr.com/blog/employee-engagement-9 -strategies-to-keep-your-remote-team-connected/

- *10 Best Practices for Building an OnlineCommunity*https://www.meltingspot.io/the-guide-to-com munity-building/best-practices-for-building-an-online-community

- 15Five.(n.d.). *Continuous performance management.* Retrieved from h ttps://www.15five.com

- *19 Tips to Improve Work-Life Balance While Working Remotely* https ://www.halfhalfhome.com/work/work-life-balance.html

- *A Guide to Corporate Mentoring Programs in2024*https://www.qoop er.io/blog/corporate-mentoring-programs

- *Applying the Agile Methodology to the ModernWorkplace*https://mobile-jon.com/2021/04/05/applying

-the-agile-methodology-to-the-modern-workplace/

- Asana.(2024). *100+ team motivational quotes for collaboration.* Retrieved from https://asana.com/resources/team-motivational-quotes

- *Authentic leadership: Definition, examples and how to develop it* https://getmarlee.com/blog/authentic-leadership

- BambooHR.(n.d.). *Employee retention and analytics.* Retrieved from https://www.bamboohr.com

- *Becoming ADisruptor: How Mastering YourCulture Can* ...https://www.forbes.com/councils/forbesbusinesscouncil/2021/10/15/becoming-a-disruptor-how-mastering-your-culture-can-help-you-stay-ahead/

- Bennett, M. (2022, May 10). *10 of the best empathetic leadership quotes from* real leaders. Niagara Institute. Retrieved from https://www.niagarainstitute.com/blog/empathetic-leadership-quotes

- BSCDesigner. (n.d.). *Balanced scorecard software.* Retrieved from https://bscdesigner.com

- *Building a Feedback-Rich Culture*https://hbr.org/2013/12/building-a-feedback-rich-culture

- *Case Studies of Successful Multicultural TeamIntegration* ...https://vorecol.com/blogs/blog-case-studies-of-successful-multicultural-team-integration-through-technology-164673

- *Case Study: Pharmaceutical Company Boosts Team...*https://www.reshift.us/articles/blog/case-study-pharmaceutical-company-boosts-team-collaborations-with-empathy-mapping-1

- *ChangeManagement in 2023: What Leaders Need to Know*https://www.vistage.com/research-center/business-leadership/20230207-change-management/

- ClearPointStrategy. (n.d.). *Balanced scorecard software comparison.* Retrieved from https://www.clearpointstrategy.com/blog/balanced-scor ecard-software-comparison

- *CompareCulture Assessment Tools*https://www.wanttoworkthere.com /cultural-assessment-tools

- *ContinuousImprovement*   *at*   *Two Companies*https://asq.org/quality-resources/articles/case-studies/conti nuous-improvement-at-two-companies?id=de3fe919c27b445fa952a9e 083910fe6

- *CorporateAccountability:*   *Articles,*   *Research, & Case Studies*https://hbswk.hbs.edu/Pages/browse.aspx?HBSTopic= Corporate%20Accountability

- Corporater.(n.d.). *Balanced scorecard software*. Retrieved fromhttps:/ /corporater.com/solution/balanced-scorecard-software/

- *Crisis*   *Management*   *and*   *Resilience in Leadership*https://www.linkedin.com/pulse/crisis-management-res ilience-leadership-kristen-mcdermott-5chce

- *Culture ChangeCase Study: Volvo IT*https://www.sweetrush.com/cult ure-change-case-study-volvo-it/

- CultureMonkey.(n.d.). *Employee engagement survey tools*. Retrieved from https://www.culturemonkey.io/employee-engagement/employe e-engagement-survey-tools/

- Deliberate Directions. (2024, July 5). *130 quotes about business comm unication.*Retrieved from https://www.deliberatedirections.com/quot es-business-communication/

- EffyAI. (2023, April 10). *50 accountability quotes for a more successful workplace*. Retrieved from https://www.effy.ai/blog/accountability-q uotes

- *EmbracingRemote*   *Work:*   *4*   *Top*   *CompaniesDeveloping* ...https://blog.bestpracticeinstitute.org/embracing-remote-work/

- *EmotionalIntelligence in Leaders: Real LifeExamples*https://envisiongloballeadership.com/blog/emotional-intelligence-leaders-real-life-examples/

- *EmotionalIntelligence Training Programs, Leadership* ...https://www.ihhp.com/emotional-intelligence-training/

- *Evolving YourCompany Culture: Adapting ToChange And* ...https://www.8figurefirm.com/evolving-your-company-culture/

- *Five Ways ToBuild Trust And PsychologicalSafety With* ...https://www.forbes.com/sites/darrenmenabney/2021/03/27/five-ways-to-build-trust-and-psychological-safety-with-your-hybrid-team/

- Glint.(n.d.). *Employee feedback and sentiment analysis platform.* Retrieved from https://www.glintinc.com

- *How AligningPersonal and Company Values Leads to Success*https://www.cultureworkshr.com/how-aligning-personal-and-company-values-leads-to-success/

- *How and WhenDoes Visionary Leadership Promote...*https://www.ncbi.nlm.nih.gov/pmc/articles/PMC9343966/

- *How Companies Can Improve Employee Engagement...*https://hbr.org/2021/10/how-companies-can-improve-employee-engagement-right-now

- *How DoesLeadership Influence OrganizationalCulture?*https://online.hbs.edu/blog/post/organizational-culture-and-leadership

- *How to align on shared team values: a workshop design* ...https://www.wayra.de/blog/how-to-align-on-shared-team-values-a-workshop-design-guide

- *How to BuildInclusion in a Hybrid WorkEnvironment*https://aperian.com/blog/inclusion-in-the-hybrid-work-world/

- *How To ScaleCulture As A Rapid-GrowthStart-Up*https://www.forbes.com/sites/kevinkruse/2023/10/19/how-to-scale-culture-as-a-rapid-growth-start-up/

- *INCLUSION& DIVERSITY CASE STUDIES*https://embracedifference.ert.eu/wp-content/uploads/2020/09/ERT_embracing_difference_V26-1.pdf

- IndeedEditorial Team. (2024, June 27). *40 change management quotes to inspire the entire team.* Indeed. Retrieved from https://ca.indeed.com/career-advice/career-development/change-management-quotes

- *LeadershipAccountability: How to Build ItInto Your Culture*https://www.betterworks.com/magazine/accountability-in-leadership/

- *Making EmpathyCentral to Your Company Culture*https://hbr.org/2019/05/making-empathy-central-to-your-company-culture

- *Managing the Cultural Pitfalls of Hybrid Work*https://sloanreview.mit.edu/article/managing-the-cultural-pitfalls-of-hybrid-work/

- *Metrics for Assessing the Success of Transformation Efforts*https://iriconsultants.com/measuring-cultural-impact-metrics-for-assessing-the-success-of-transformation-efforts/

- OfficeRnD.(2023, January 17). *12 intriguing hybrid work quotes from successful leaders.*Retrieved from https://www.officernd.com/blog/hybrid-work-quotes/

- *Overcoming theTop 5 Barriers to Diversity andInclusion*https://cloud.name-coach.com/overcoming-barriers-to-diversity-and-inclusion/

- *PreventingEmployee Burnout in a Hybrid World*https://www.chiefofstaff.network/blog/preventing-employee-burnout-in-a-hybrid-world

- *Proven Tactics for Improving Teams'Psychological Safety*https://sloanreview.mit.edu/article/proven-tactics-for-improving-teams-psychological-safety/

- Qualtrics.(n.d.). *Employeeengagement surveys.* Retrieved from https://www.qualtrics.com/experience-management/employee/employee-engagement-survey/

- Reiner, A. (2024, July 5). *Leadership quotes.* Word Counter. Retrieved from https://word-counter.com/popular/leadership-quotes/

- SurveyMonkey.(n.d.). *Employee surveys.* Retrieved from https://www.surveymonkey.com/mp/employee-surveys/

- TeamBuilding.(2024, February 13). *70 powerful diversity and inclusion quotes for* the workplace. Retrieved from https://teambuilding.com/blog/diversity-and-inclusion-quotes

- *The Case forEmotionally Intelligent Leaders*https://www.kornferry.com/insights/briefings-magazine/issue-64/the-case-for-emotionally-intelligent-leaders

- *The CriticalRole Technology Plays in CompanyCulture*https://www.reworked.co/digital-workplace/the-critical-role-technology-plays-to-support-company-culture/

- *The Future of the Office Has Arrived: It'sHybrid*https://www.gallup.com/workplace/511994/future-office-arrived-hybrid.aspx

- *The Influence of Company Culture On Employee...*https://www.holaspirit.com/blog/influence-company-culture-on-employee-engagement

- *The Power OfVulnerability In Leadership: Experts Say ...*https://www.forbes.com/sites/luisromero/2023/03/08/the-power-of-vulnerability-in-leadership-experts-say-authenticity-and-honesty-can-move-people-and-achieve-results/

- *The Role ofEmpathy in Driving SuccessfulChange Initiatives*https://www.acldigital.com/blogs/role-empathy-driving-successful-change-initiatives

- *The Role of Leadership in Fostering WorkplaceDiversity and ...*https://blog.bib.com/blog/the-role-of-leadership-in-fostering-workplace-diversity-and-inclusion#:~:text=Leaders%20play%20a%20critical%20role,employees%20bring%20to%20the%20table.

- *Top 5Strategies for Creating an Inclusive Workplace (2023)*https://www.aqore.com/strategies-for-creating-an-inclusive-workplace/

- *ValuesMisalignment at Work: A Case Study*https://www.wearekadabra.com/values-misalignment-at-work-a-case-study/

- Vantage Circle. (n.d.). *100 thought-provoking company culture quotes.*Retrieved November 21, 2024, from https://www.vantagecircle.com/en/blog/company-culture-quotes/

- Workday.(n.d.). *Humancapital management software.* Retrieved from https://www.workday.com

Made in United States
Troutdale, OR
03/07/2025

29563146R00080